WORKPLACE FABLES

147 true-life stories

workplacefables.com

WORKPLACE FABLES

147 true-life stories

MARK PRICE

STOUR
PUBLISHING

An imprint of
David Fickling Books

Published in Great Britain in 2017 by Stour Publishing

An imprint of David Fickling Books
31 Beaumont Street, Oxford, OX1 2NP

www.davidficklingbooks.com

Text © Mark Price, 2017
Cover illustration © Noma Bar, 2017
Interior illustrations © Nick Hayes, 2017

ISBN 978-1-910200-78-0

1 3 5 7 9 10 8 6 4 2

Papers used by David Fickling Books are from
well-managed forests and other responsible sources.

To my father for the lessons he taught me
about business in my childhood years.

To Brian O'Callaghan, my first Managing Director,
who so generously gave me and others so much of his
time and helped us to understand and grow.

CONTENTS

WORKPLACE FABLES

Illustrated by Nick Hayes

IN HOMAGE
TO AESOP

A young rabbit played with his brothers and sisters in the lush grass outside their burrow, enjoying the warmth of the spring sun. The silence was shattered when the rabbit's mother, standing on guard, twitched her nose and shouted, 'Run, run! Fox, fox!'

The young rabbits turned to see a large fox creeping up on them under the cover of the tall meadow grass on the slope below their burrow. Whilst the young rabbit's siblings screamed and ran he hopped calmly back towards the small hole they called home.

The big old fox saw the young rabbit moving slowly after his brothers and sisters, who were already almost underground. *What a silly young rabbit*, thought the fox. *He'll be my breakfast!* And he ran as fast as he could to catch him. But the youngster disappeared into the tiny hole just as the fox leaped to catch his prey. The fox, in his haste, had misjudged the size of the hole and instead of ensnaring his prey, trapped his snout in the small opening to the burrow.

How the rabbits laughed at the old fox for not better judging the size of the hole. From the safety of their burrow they pulled at the fox's whiskers and sang how clever their young brother was to know the fox would not fit in their burrow and how very stupid the fox was.

When the fox was able to pull his snout out he was very sore and cross indeed. 'I'll show that young rabbit,' he murmured and moved to the top of the bank, down-wind from the burrow, where he waited and waited. Eventually at sunset the rabbits decided to go out again to play. 'The old fox will be long gone now. He is after all very stupid,' boasted the young rabbit to his brothers and sisters.

Tentative at first, they emerged from their lair. Becoming more confident, as there was neither sight nor scent of the fox, they moved into the meadow to play.

The fox waited patiently but it wasn't long before the young rabbit was far enough from his burrow for the fox to pounce. He moved like lightning from his hiding place to catch and eat him.

'How stupid he was,' said the fox. 'Did he really not know that I would wait to have my fill!'

What is easy and obvious to one is not to another.
Never think someone stupid for not knowing
something you do.

INTRODUCTION

From the youngest age I remember working. My father used to own a small grocers shop before I was born, and then, when I was small, left his job at the large biscuit company where he was a salesman to open his own wholesale business. He saw there was a gap in the market, as the big suppliers would only deal in large orders which left small shops, schools and leisure centres struggling for supply. His plan was to buy in bulk and supply these smaller businesses.

Before and after school I would help unload lorries and fill vans. I would travel with him in my school holidays. He'd have me do mental maths to calculate prices, test me on the names of customers and their children and encourage me to talk to the people we visited.

As a Christian and a part-time preacher my father had pretty clear views on business and life. He believed that in the eyes of God everyone was equal, that there could be no profit in prejudice and that small acts of kindness would always pay off.

I remember once visiting a young man who had just opened a tiny shop. He told my father he couldn't afford a full box of biscuits to sell, and so was incredibly grateful when my dad said he would split a box and take payment next time to get the new shopkeeper started. Even at a young age I saw how clever my father had been to hook a new customer. But when we got home and unloaded the van my father noticed that instead of giving the shopkeeper twelve packs of biscuits from the box of twenty-four he had, in fact, only given him eleven. Against my protestations, at the end of a long day, he insisted we drive the twenty miles or so back to the little shop and give the man the packet we had shorted him by. He knew how important that one packet would be to someone starting out. The young man was very grateful for my father's honesty, kindness and humanity. That small act ensured that as his business grew, and he opened a chain of shops, he stayed loyal to my father to supply him, even though he may have got better prices straight from the large manufacturer once he had the scale.

These, and many other lessons I learned from my father,

I took into my adult working life. After finishing my university degree, I was very privileged to spend the next thirty-three years employed by John Lewis and Waitrose. I worked at every level from shop floor to boardroom, and for most of that time served as Managing Director of Waitrose and latterly also as Deputy Chairman of the John Lewis Partnership. The John Lewis Partnership, for those of you who don't know it, is a very different kind of business, owned by all of those that work in it, and therefore requiring a particularly thoughtful type of management. During my years in the business I worked for seven Managing Directors and three Chairmen, and with more managers than I could ever count, each unique and with very different styles of management. Along the way I have run retail businesses and marketing, IT, and development and strategy functions. I have had the good fortune to chair charities and trade bodies and sit on other boards. And I have watched eagle-eyed at all my competitors and what other businesses have done.

All of which is the longest preamble to say that the fables in this book are true. I have diligently collected them throughout my career. Many are personal experiences while others I either heard of or read about and were too good to leave out!

While the scenarios are true, the identifying details have been changed. The moral that accompanies each fable is the lesson I have taken from them. I hope you find the stories interesting, amusing and, perhaps, I hope, of some help to you.

CHAPTER ONE

Starting out

THE RELUCTANT BUSINESSWOMAN AND THE LIFE LESSON

'I don't think I would be any good at business,' said the Reluctant Businesswoman.

The young lady was speaking with her father, who was himself a successful businessman. They were discussing her career options as she neared the end of her education.

'Why don't you think you'd be any good?' asked her father.

'It all seems so complicated and difficult, I really don't think I could do it,' she replied.

'But you got the job in the local coffee shop even though lots of people applied,' said her father.

'That's not business,' replied the Reluctant Businesswoman.

'And you persuaded your teacher to go with your project idea, even though he was reluctant at first,' he went on.

'But that's not business,' came the reply.

'And you sold your sister your old phone, remember?' smiled her father.

'But that's not business,' she repeated.

'Then you lent your mother money for her new dress in

exchange for a cup of coffee and cake, didn't you?,' her father continued.

'Rocky Road,' replied the young woman.

'It will be!' laughed her father, 'and you will need a lot of determination and energy but you see, the art of business is about making people want what you have. Successful business people are better at doing that. And I think you have a real gift for it!'

All business and life is about selling –
oneself, ideas, money, buildings, things.

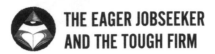

THE EAGER JOBSEEKER AND THE TOUGH FIRM

The Eager Jobseeker was very keen to get onto a graduate training program. After applying to dozens of businesses, in every industry, she was successful in getting an interview with a high-profile and very commercially aggressive organisation called Lynchem Associates.

Before the interview the Eager Jobseeker did her homework. She was a little alarmed by Lynchem Associates tough reputation and the stories about its hire-and-fire culture, the fierce ambition of its staff and the iron discipline exacted by its executives.

Hang on, she thought, *to get this job I am going to need to present myself as being ruthless and driven.*

The Eager Jobseeker was so keen to get a job, she immediately began searching her memory for examples of where she had displayed these extreme behaviour traits. It was difficult, and so where they didn't exist, she twisted the truth to present herself in the best light to the employer.

The Eager Jobseeker's approach worked and she was offered a role on the graduate program. But, within weeks, she started to feel very uncomfortable with how employees were pushed and bullied to achieve targets. She hated how unrelenting she and her colleagues were expected to be with suppliers.

After an unhappy year she and Lynchem Associates parted company.

> *Always be yourself in an interview and in your job.*
> *That way you will ensure the right fit.*

THE RIGHT FIT?

The StaffPick recruitment agency prided itself on placing new recruits into the right jobs. It had an eye-wateringly complex computer resourcing system that scored applicants on a range of criteria, from their educational qualifications, to previous experience, to hobbies and interests.

One day a prospective client came to look over StaffPick to see if they would be suitable to take on the job of recruiting a large new team for his business.

'Let me introduce you to one of our success stories,' crowed the StaffPick executive charged with impressing the Prospective Client.

The Prospective Client was introduced to a young lady who had just secured a job behind the fish counter at a local store.

'She has a Ph.D in marine biology and achieved a whale of a score on our computer system,' the StaffPick executive boasted. 'She's perfect for the job because there is little she doesn't know about fish. Quite a catch I'd say.'

The Prospective Client wished the marine biologist well and continued his tour, before going on his way.

Later that day, the Prospective Client called to thank StaffPick but said he would be taking his business elsewhere.

'But why?' asked the StaffPick executive, who was genuinely mystified.

'That marine biologist, she'll be gone in less than six months,' said the Prospective Client. 'It is most unlikely that a new recruit with qualifications like that would want a career on a shop fish counter. She is simply biding time until what she wants comes along. By taking on such a person, the shop will incur extra costs. Meanwhile, with care a more suitable candidate could have been recruited who is interested in building a long-term career in food retail.'

And he was right, the marine biologist floated away in less than two months.

Don't get confused about the attributes
a successful candidate needs.

THE OBSERVANT TRAINEE
WHO NOTICED THINGS

Every year the bosses at Vastway would take on a dozen new trainees and eagerly monitor their progress. Competition was high among the trainees to see who would catch the eye of those at the top at Vastway to become Trainee of the Year and be guaranteed fast-track promotion.

This particular year was no different.

It's bound to be me, thought the trainee who had achieved the highest-ever academic score in the tests they all took before they joined.

But it wasn't.

I'll get in at 6am and never leave before 9pm, thought the most hardworking and diligent trainee. *It's bound to be me.*

But she wasn't the most successful trainee either.

I'll make coffee for everyone, every day, thought the most ingratiating trainee. *It's bound to be me.*

But that didn't work.

Remarkably, it was not the most academic, nor the most hardworking, or diligent, or the most confident trainees that progressed faster than the others. The trainee who caught everybody's attention had two gifts that no one else seemed to have: he noticed things and then, when he did, he did something about them, without any fuss.

The Observant Trainee noticed when people looked upset or happy and either consoled or celebrated with them.

He noticed when things were missing, or needed tidying, or more manpower was required. Then the Observant Trainee would work with his team to do what was needed.

Whenever anyone spoke about him, they said the Observant Trainee was exceptionally bright, hardworking, pleasant and on-the ball.

In reality, he was no more so than anyone else. The Observant Trainee simply had the talent for noticing things.

See what needs to be done and then do it.
This is the most important management skill.

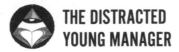

THE DISTRACTED YOUNG MANAGER

After a busy festive season in the Golden Apple store's Christmas department, the Temporary Worker was looking forward to a hard-earned rest. She'd worked long hours, seven days a week, for nearly two months.

The Christmas department manager told the Temporary Worker there was just one job left to do: the Christmas department stocktake.

'It's not very complicated, but it needs to be accurate,' the Young Manager explained. 'We've got a schoolkid on work experience here this week too, so I have asked him to help you.'

The Temporary Worker and the Work Experience Student set about the task, packing the leftover Christmas trees, baubles and cards into boxes and recording what was in each one on stock sheets. The Young Manager left them both to it while he wrote a report to Golden Apple head office about how sparkling Christmas trading had been, in order to get himself noticed.

After a few days, the Temporary Worker and her work experience assistant had boxed everything up, and put the boxes on the warehouse shelves and handed the Young Manager the stock sheets. Still busy polishing his glossy report and carefully considering what binding would be best, he sent the stock sheets straight to his finance department and later presented his report to the Managing Director's office.

When the stock sheets were checked some weeks later, pandemonium broke out. The boxes had not been numbered and it was impossible to reconcile what was inside with what was on the sheets. When the boxes were opened, the stock was found to have been put in haphazardly. The Temporary Worker had not known to bundle goods up by price point or description. The entire job had to be done again and the good reputation the Young Manager had achieved over a successful Christmas was lost.

Without supervision and clear instruction,
tasks will only be completed to the best ability
of the most experienced on the job.

THE TRAINEE MANAGER AND THE BIG MISTAKE

No one could accuse the Trainee Manager of a lack of enthusiasm. What he lacked in knowledge, he made up for with eagerness, zeal and devotion to the job. As he moved from department to department in the Great Value supermarket head office, he took an intense interest in learning about all aspects of the business.

One day, the Trainee Manager was very excited to be joining the buying department of Great Value. He lapped up all there was to know about ordering goods and allocating them to the shops.

Everything was going swimmingly until the Trainee Manager became distracted when placing an order. Instead of buying fifty cases of chicken wings, he ordered five hundred!

Inevitably, the shops were overwhelmed with chicken wings. They were soon on the phone to head office crying foul. Hundreds of cases of unsold chicken wings had to be destroyed. The mistake cost Great Value a lot of money.

The Trainee Manager felt very low. He felt even worse when the Managing Director, who was abreast of the problem, arrived to talk to him.

The Trainee Manager barely gave the Managing Director time to speak, and having plucked up the courage blurted out, 'I have cost the company tens of thousands of pounds in unnecessary wastage, lost the confidence of the shops, buyers and finance teams and I would therefore like to resign!'

'Don't be silly,' said the Managing Director. 'I have spent tens of thousands of pounds training you. Why would I now want that experience to go elsewhere!

'What I need you to do is to put in place procedures to make sure nobody can ever make the same mistake again. If you can do that this experience has been good for you and for the business.'

Mistakes, well managed, are often a good way
for individuals and companies to improve.

THE LISTENING MANAGER
AND THE NEW RECRUIT

The New Recruit felt very despondent. She'd joined the parcel delivery firm Deliverist with high hopes only a short while before, but now she'd been posted to a new department in disgrace.

She'd been put on probation just because she had not moved quickly enough in doing what her boss asked for. He'd screamed that she was utterly useless for not doing precisely what he asked, when he asked it, and even worse, she'd had the temerity to answer back, and so he moved her on .

The Probationer slunk over to her desk in her new department and concentrated on making herself invisible.

'Hello,' said the Listening Manager. 'Welcome to the department. Could you please process these orders straight away?'

The Probationer took a big gulp. Her heart was hammering in her chest. How could she point out the problem with the request, without being fired altogether this time?

'I'm afraid I can't,' the Probationer said quietly, just waiting for a volley of abuse to come back.

But she was surprised when her manager simply asked: 'Why?'

'I have to finish these invoices first,' the Probationer explained. 'If I don't pay them by 10 o'clock Deliverist will lose its discount.'

'That's a pretty good reason.' The Listening Manager smiled. 'When do you think you can process the orders by?'

'I should be able to do them after ten,' replied the Probationer, relaxing a little.

'That's brilliant,' exclaimed the Listening Manager. 'Thank you. It's so good to have someone in the department with your experience.'

The Probationer felt good and worked hard to keep getting the Listening Manager's praise. She turned into one of the best workers in the office and her probation was lifted.

Asking rather than telling often
brings greater results.

THE IMPATIENT GRADUATE TRAINEE AND THE ELUSIVE PROMOTION

The Impatient Graduate Trainee was frustrated and annoyed to be the last of his peer group to be promoted. His moaning reached the ears of the Managing Director, who called him to his office.

'I think I have done a far better job than some of those promoted ahead of me,' complained the Impatient Graduate Trainee. 'They are having much better careers than me.'

The Managing Director asked the Impatient Graduate Trainee what job he aspired to do.

'I want to be the CEO and I want to get there quickly,' the Impatient Graduate Trainee said confidently.

'Well, the average tenure of a CEO is five years, so how old do you want to be when you start your five years?' the Managing Director asked.

This question made the Impatient Graduate Trainee pause to think for a while.

'When I am about forty-five I suppose,' he said at last.

'So, if you become a CEO when you are forty-five, will you judge the next twenty-three years between now and then a failure?' the Managing Director pressed. 'Rather than be in such a mad rush, you should use the time to learn and enjoy the experience. At each step be the best you can be. Cream always rises to the top!'

Be patient. A career is judged over a lifetime.

THE ATTENTIVE AND INATTENTIVE MANAGERS AND THE DISAPPEARING TALENT

One day, when reviewing their graduate training success rates, the bosses at Counter Balance made a startling discovery. Trainees who were seconded to Department Sore invariably quit the programme just a short while after finishing. However, those who went to Department See, generally stayed at Counter Balance to develop their careers.

What was happening? Counter Balance bosses dug deeper to find out.

In Department Sore, where people were leaving, they discovered the Inattentive Manager there left the trainees to learn on the job. Despite all the evidence, the Inattentive Manager was utterly convinced that this was the right approach. He was too busy and impatient for success to spend time with trainees. He'd let them know when things had gone wrong and they would learn from that. In Department See, the Attentive Manager would see the trainees for a quick chat each day and a full meeting each week. This constant interest and nurturing kept them engaged and eager.

After that, all Counter Balance graduates were placed

with hands on, nurturing managers who took an interest and engaged with them. Talent blossomed.

Left without attention, the best will leave.

THE FOOTBALL AGENT
AND THE WHIZZ KID

The Football Agent went to see the Head Coach to talk about his players.

'Ok, what have you got for me?' asked the Head Coach.

'Two midfielders,' said the Football Agent. 'One is twenty-five and has had a good season for his club. He can see a pass, has a good engine and covers the ground. All in all, a determined player, worthy of the top flight.'

'I know him, he's good, what's the price?' enquired the Head Coach.

'£3 million and great value for it,' said the Football Agent.

'And your other player?' asked the Head Coach.

'Wow, he is special,' enthused the Football Agent. 'Only seventeen and also a midfielder. This one has only played a handful of games though. He glides over the grass, scored a stunning goal in his second game and is eager to learn. I think he will have it all. England class in my view.'

'Sounds good,' said the Head Coach, leaning in. 'How much?'

'£10 million,' said the Football Agent without missing a beat.

'But how can he cost three times more than the proven good player?' asked the Head Coach in disbelief.

'Because of what he could be,' replied the Football Agent.

*Potential is one of the most valuable
commodities in business.*

CHAPTER TWO

Ambition – A good servant,
but a bad master

THE AMBITIOUS MANAGER'S JOURNEY

The Ambitious Manager at Penrose Steep leaned back in his comfy office chair and sighed with pleasure. He was sad to leave his old team behind, but was very pleased with his new promotion. He had wanted to be promoted so much. As he thought about all the things he could do now, he was suddenly overwhelmed with the feeling he wasn't quite happy enough. *No*, the Ambitious Manager thought, *I won't be truly fulfilled until I achieve my next promotion to become a department manager.*

So, the Ambitious Manager threw himself into his new role, built a great team, enjoyed the best results ever at Penrose Steep and was lauded by his colleagues.

Sure enough after a few years hard work, the Ambitious Manager was promoted to department manager.

His team threw a farewell party to celebrate and the Ambitious Manager told everyone how happy he was, both with his own achievement and also that of his team. Deep down though, the feeling of pleasure and fulfilment at his promotion was already beginning to ebb away.

If only I could become a general manager, he thought. *Now that really would make me happy.*

The Ambitious Manager worked even harder to achieve his goal. He stayed late at night, worked at weekends and took few holidays. He never complained because he loved his work and the team he built. His team never complained either because they loved and respected the department manager.

No one was surprised when, after a couple of years, the Ambitious Manager won the promotion to general manager of Penrose Steep. He was thrilled and opened a big bottle of champagne to celebrate with everyone. *Surely now I will be satisfied*, he thought to himself.

On the Ambitious Manager's first day as a general manager he reflected on how well he had done as he sat alone in his large office. Then, a familiar empty feeling started to spread in the pit of his stomach.

I know I will feel completely satisfied when I become managing director, he thought, preparing himself for another few years of hard graft.

> *It is the journey, not the destination,*
> *which brings real happiness.*

THE INEXPERIENCED MANAGER AND THE LIGHTS

Everyone knew the Lighthouse lighting shop. It had been a feature of the High Street for many years. Many adults remembered standing on the street outside as children, staring transfixed by the intricate crystal chandeliers that were arrayed across the large picture windows at the front of Lighthouse.

One day, an Inexperienced Manager took over. He too had known the shop since he was a young boy but this was the first time he'd really spent any time inside.

He walked around, doing his best to plug the gaps in his knowledge by getting to know the stock.

When he reached the back of the store, the Inexperienced Manager was surprised to find an array of modern lighting. It came from a different era completely from the old-fashioned crystal chandeliers in the front.

I wonder why it is not displayed more prominently, the Inexperienced Manager thought. *Surely this is more what people want to buy?*

The Inexperienced Manager watched the customers carefully in his first week at the lighting shop. He saw that it was a small core of older customers that adored the expensive chandelier display but he only sold a couple that week. However, many more younger customers made a bee-line for the fashionable modern lighting at the back of the shop. *Illuminating,* he thought.

That weekend the Inexperienced Manager seized the initiative and worked overtime to switch the store around. The crystal chandeliers were squeezed into the back recesses of the shop, while a display of bright modern lights was set up in the picture window.

The following week, sales of all lighting plummeted. Although the manager sold more inexpensive modern lights, the loyal older customers thought that the shop no longer sold the expensive chandeliers, so went elsewhere and those that did venture in were disappointed to find chandeliers packed together at the back of the shop. The magic had all but disappeared. Pretty soon, so did the profits.

Understand where you get your biggest returns before being distracted by the new and less profitable.

 ## THE SMUG SHOPKEEPER AND THE GIANT STORE

The Smug Shopkeeper was proud of his huge new shop, Jumbo Jinx.

'We sell everything here,' he boasted loudly. 'There is nothing I have not thought of. There is everything you could buy in any one of the shops on the High Street and yet, here it is, all under one roof.'

The Smug Shopkeeper stood back and waited for the hordes of shoppers to beat a path to the door of Jumbo Jinx. And waited. And waited.

But hardly anybody came.

Aghast, the Smug Shopkeeper walked out onto the High Street and collared the first shopper he saw scurrying past.

'Why are you not shopping at my giant store?' he demanded. 'We have everything you need and more.'

'Oh, I took a look but I didn't think your range was as good as so-and-so over there,' said the startled shopper, hurrying on.

The Smug Shopkeeper grabbed another shopper and asked the same question.

'Well, your prices are good, but they are not as good as so-and-so's,' the shopper blurted out, before dashing off.

Each shopper the Smug Shopkeeper asked seemed to have a different reason.

The service was not as fast as so-and-so.

The quality was not as good as so-and-so.

The Smug Shopkeeper shook his head sadly and returned to his large, empty, store.

More is not always better. The sum of the parts does not guarantee your success, each area must succeed on its own merits.

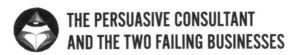

THE PERSUASIVE CONSULTANT
AND THE TWO FAILING BUSINESSES

There were once two businesses, Clockwise and Anti-Clockwise. Neither of them was doing very well. Both were losing customers and market share, and both were going nowhere fast. The managers at each business scrabbled around, looking for ways to cut costs, but nothing much seemed to make a difference and the two companies continued to lose money.

One day, a Persuasive Consultant came along and told the managers at Clockwise and Anti-Clockwise that he had a great idea.

'Wouldn't it be great if these companies merged, so they could share just one office?' he said. 'You could cut your costs, reduce your workforce and benefit from higher combined sales.'

The respective managers thought this sounded like a fantastic idea and paid the Persuasive Consultant a huge fee to show them exactly how to merge the companies and cut their costs. The bank was very encouraging, since it was also able to renegotiate its fees as a result of the change and take a large commission on the merger. The shareholders were also keen, since they also imagined they might make some money.

And so it came to pass that two failing businesses became one huge failing business, which spun out of control and closed not long after the Persuasive Consultant, banks, resourceful managers and shareholders had taken their money generated on the back of nothing more than pure optimism.

Two bad businesses never make a good one –
but remember, the greedy never care.

THE MARKETING WHIZZ AND THE CARS

Everyone at the Vroomsy car factory was very excited when the Marketing Whizz joined. He had a reputation for being a very clever, creative man.

On his first day, he accelerated onto the factory floor and announced an audacious plan for the sleepy automotive company.

'Right,' he boomed confidently. 'We are going to grow this company. However, we are not going to grow by 5 per cent a year. No, we are going to grow by 25 per cent!

'It will be the biggest and best promotional campaign ever seen,' went on the Marketing Whizz. 'Vroomsy will blow the competition away. The extra cars we sell will more than cover the cost of the marketing campaign and promotional discounts.'

Everybody was excited, except for the Production Manager who was listening at the back. He knew they would need to run the factory 24/7 to increase production to meet this demand. They'd also need to buy extra space for the stock and persuade the car showrooms to order more in advance. Plus, all the smaller companies who supplied the factory would need extra financing to build more capacity, to employ additional staff and to buy more stock. It would be a big financial risk. But no one wanted to listen to the Production Manager because he wasn't delivering an exciting message of huge growth. The Marketing Whizz went ahead with his plans. The new adverts were created, production increased by a third and car dealers were encouraged to order more.

The factory struggled under the strain, but sales began to take off. Vroomsy bosses were delighted and hailed the Marketing Whizz as a genius. Never had a car manufacturer seen this scale of growth before.

Sadly though, sales never reached the promised 25 per cent. They stuck stubbornly at 15 per cent. Soon everyone got very disillusioned and fed up that the target had been missed by such a huge margin. Worse still, the company made huge losses on the unsold cars and was unable to pay its smaller suppliers, who went bankrupt.

The Marketing Whizz was asked to leave and the Production Manager took on the job of delivering sustainable profits and sales.

Under-promise and over-deliver.

THE IMPATIENT SUPPLIER
AND THE BIGGER FIRM

The Impatient Supplier had been dealing with just one store for many years. Things were going well with the Neighbourly Shop Group, but they weren't particularly dynamic. The Impatient Supplier grew restless and began to look around for new opportunities to make more money.

'I need to sell to more shops,' the Impatient Supplier resolved. 'That will push up our income.'

The Impatient Supplier went out on the road and spoke to many stores. Remarkably, within a short space of time, he managed to negotiate a deal to supply Rollback, the Neighbourly Shop Group's biggest rival with more than twice the number of outlets. To secure the deal with Rollback, the Impatient Supplier had to offer the bigger firm a much larger discount, but he put it down as the price of expansion.

When the Impatient Supplier's original customer, the Neighbourly Shop Group, saw the size of the discount on offer to their rival, they were furious. They didn't even bother trying to renegotiate their own deal. They decided the Impatient Supplier had no loyalty, so they no longer wanted to do business with him and ended their long-standing agreement.

To make matters, worse the Impatient Supplier's products did not sell very well at Rollback's shops. They too decided to stop selling them.

Now the Impatient Supplier had no customers at all.

It is hard to serve two masters.

THE FOOLISH SUPPLIER
WITH TOO MUCH STOCK

There was once a company that sold very fine beef to an upmarket store chain. Shoppers loved the good-quality meat and were happy to pay premium prices to get it, especially since there was nothing like it anywhere else.

One day, the beef company found that it had more meat than the upmarket retailer required. A discount chain buyer heard a rumour about the overstock and called the beef producer. He was put straight through to the Foolish Supplier.

'You have all that extra beef and it will go to waste if you don't sell it,' the discounter wheedled. 'Why don't I take it off your hands at cost price? Then at least you won't lose any cash.'

The Foolish Supplier was easily seduced by the suggestion and agreed to the deal.

Naturally, the discount shop was very pleased with their coup. They couldn't help but advertise the fact that they were now selling the same beef as the upmarket shop, but at a much lower cost. Sales at the discount shop soared and everyone started talking about it. Very soon, the upmarket chain's customers began to accuse them of ripping them off for years!

The bosses at the upmarket retailer were furious. Overnight, they cancelled their contract with the producer.

The Foolish Supplier turned to the discounter, in a bid to form a new long-term relationship.

'Of course,' smiled the discount chain buyer. 'But we will need to negotiate a lower price to reflect our terms of business.'

Beware of offering vastly different deals to competing companies. It will always end badly.

THE EGOTISTICAL EXECUTIVE WHO MANAGED UP

Everyone knew the chief executive of the Triplico holiday company would be retiring soon. It was all anyone in the firm could talk about, and most importantly, who would succeed him?

There only seemed to be two credible candidates. Both executives had a good track record, drive and ambition. There was little to choose between them.

The first candidate, the Egotistical Executive, decided the best way to get the top job was to manage up. He spent his days pandering to the needs of the handful of people on the Triplico board who would decide who the next boss should be.

His rival executive believed the opposite, that managing down was the key. He thought his time and energy were best spent on those working for him and that results would speak for themselves and sway the bosses.

When the time came, the Egotistical Executive won hands down. The entire board decided he was the perfect man for the job.

As soon as he took up his position, the Egotistical Executive turned his attention to the next step in his career progression. He barely gave the team below him a second thought. Soon, the entire company became divided and unsettled. At the first opportunity they staged a coup in an attempt to unseat their hated new leader.

The Egotistical Executive didn't care. He simply left to run another business, which was persuaded of his credentials by the fact he had got to the top job at Triplico.

Meanwhile the executive who managed down finally got the job at Triplico. He continued to nurture and support his team. The team united and supported the new chief executive through thick and thin. Triplico enjoyed great success.

Just managing up will only bring short-term
success and you will be found out.

THE FLEXIBLE AND THE STUBBORN MANAGERS AND THE NEW PLAN

There were once two managers who worked for the Talk More telephone giant. They ran separate divisions within the group, were hugely successful and understood their businesses well. They each also believed passionately that they were following the right strategy.

At Talk More head office the top executives cast an eye over their firm and wondered aloud whether the managers were in fact following the best possible strategy. The head office people were nowhere near as experienced as the two managers on the ground, but felt they had a lot to contribute nevertheless.

'Perhaps they are too close to things,' the head office people mused.

After agreeing they were going to involve themselves more, the experts at head office summoned the two managers. They wanted to tell them about the new direction they needed to follow.

Both of the managers immediately disagreed with many of the new ideas, believing strongly that Talk More would be better off if they were able to continue running their divisions as they wanted and believed best. However, the two managers had a very different way of dealing with the intervention.

The Flexible Manager went into the boardroom, listened to what head office had to say and declared he largely agreed with them. He felt satisfied that if he played along, he'd still be able to do 90 per cent of what he wanted. Satisfied they had been listened to, the head office executives sent the Flexible Manager back to his post where he continued much as before, largely unencumbered.

The Stubborn Manager decided to stick to his guns. He knew what was best in his division and said as much to his bosses when they met. There was to be no compromise. Seeing that the Stubborn Manager intended to disregard their plans completely, the bosses made it clear he would have to leave Talk More.

Sometimes it is better to adapt than be
stubborn and dig your heels in.

 THE ASPIRATIONAL EXECUTIVE AND THE JOB THAT WASN'T WHAT HE THOUGHT

The Aspirational Executive often thought about what life would be like once he had the top job at his firm. He day-dreamed about how he would tell people what to do and how they would leap to get it done. He imagined setting out a clear strategy for growth, which everyone would immediately understand and follow unquestioningly, pushing the company to new heights never-before realised.

Now that he had this picture in mind, the Aspirational Executive was determined to prove to everyone that he could be the best and get the top job. Every ounce of his energy and focus went into achieving his goal.

Eventually, the Aspirational Executive was successful and was appointed the boss of his firm. Once he got the job, he discovered it wasn't anything like he imagined at all. Not one bit. Rather than just being in charge and telling people what to do, he needed to achieve things through his managers. And, as he discovered, his managers had egos that needed to be nurtured and had to be given space in which to operate.

The Aspirational Executive discovered the top job was

more about giving his team the support to perform. He had to create a cooperative working environment, rather than running things as he had wanted to do.

The Aspirational Executive unhappily completed his time, always disappointed and wishing the job was something it wasn't.

*It's great to plan for the future, but make sure you
fully understand what your aspirations involve.*

CHAPTER THREE

Striking a balance

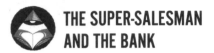 ## THE SUPER-SALESMAN
AND THE BANK

There was no one on the High Street who knew more about selling than the Super-Salesman. Every day he came up with ideas to help his customers spend more money. Store managers at the Super-Slick Supermarket marvelled at the fact people would come in expecting to spend a few pounds, yet leave having spent many times that amount. Sales promotions, two-for-one offers, buy-one-get-one free, you name it and the Super-Salesman was behind it.

The bosses at Big Bank couldn't help but notice the Super-Salesman. Not much had changed in banking for years and customers never ever parted with more cash than they had to. In fact, they'd rather have banking for free.

'What if we gave Super-Salesman a job here?' the Big Bank bosses asked. 'He could work his sales magic at the bank.'

The Super-Salesman was persuaded to leave Super-Slick Supermarket because, as well as his large salary, he was promised a bonus for each extra sale he made at Big Bank. Not surprisingly, he accepted.

Sell, sell, sell was his mantra and pretty soon he completely shook up Big Bank. Customers were flocking to sign up for his great ideas: loans, mortgages, credit cards and insurance.

The bosses at Big Bank couldn't believe how clever they had been. They were very happy indeed and so was the Super-Salesman, who banked his biggest-ever bonus cheque.

No one stopped to think that discounted milk, eggs and beans are paid for there and then, whereas financial products are paid back over years and years.

One day, the economy went into recession. Customers who had been incentivised to sign up for financial products they couldn't afford went into debt. Businesses suffered because people spent less and lots of people lost their jobs. Assets had to be written down and Big Bank lost loads of money.

'Isn't this terrible?' said the Big Bank bosses. 'All these silly people over-stretched themselves.'

A successful approach built in one business
doesn't necessarily transfer to another.

THE FIXER WITH A SWAGGER

Sinks had a problem. The plumbing company was in trouble, sales were down, customers were deserting in droves and no one seemed to have a plan to save the business from going down the drain. A succession of executives had presided over poor sales, stagnant profits and worsening public sentiment about Sinks.

One day, a confident new recruit arrived at the company. He said he liked to be called The Fixer.

'I can fix your problem: I have a plan,' said The Fixer.

'Great,' said Sinks's chairman. 'If you can grow sales again we will give you a big bonus.'

The Fixer quickly got to work. He began by dropping prices and, like many new managers, writing off as much as he could in his first year. Profits halved, but everyone held on, because The Fixer promised things would improve shortly.

The Fixer opened lots of new outlets and, sure enough, Sinks's sales grew steadily and The Fixer reaped his large bonus.

As the years rolled on, The Fixer continued to open new outlets and offices and sales continued to grow. Profits, on the other hand, were not so forthcoming as customers had become used to the lower prices but the costs of running the business had grown dramatically.

Many years on and Sinks was still only making the same level of profit that it had enjoyed when The Fixer came on board, despite its greatly increased sales. No one seemed to notice, though, and when The Fixer eventually stepped down, so he could go and help another troubled company, he did so with the praise of shareholders ringing in his ears.

'What an exceptional growth story,' they glowed. 'What a terrific business mind.'

Of course, things were not as easy for The Fixer's successor. When the market took its inevitable cyclical downturn, he had little profit to play with. Sinks returned to the doldrums and the shareholders called for the return of The Fixer.

> *Sales are not everything. Profit and balance-sheet*
> *strength are essential for long-term success.*

THE BOLD BUSINESSMAN,
THE NEW BUYER AND THE HELICOPTER

The Bold Businessman often used to boast to his friends that he knew the secret of how to get to the top: hard work.

'And good relationships,' he'd add, with a knowing wink.

Sure enough, as he worked day and night to build his small business into a large one, he never forgot to give his clients the best service imaginable. He was always there on the end on the phone, would never fail to go the extra mile and went about his business with good humour and wisdom. Every month or so, he took out the buyers of all the businesses he serviced and entertained them lavishly and built good working relationships.

The hard work paid off and the Bold Businessman became rich and successful. He decided he would kick back a little and enjoy the fruits of his labour. After all, he was running an established business.

One day, the buyer at one of his main clients retired. The Bold Businessman took him out for a goodbye meal to thank him for all his business.

'I'll introduce you to my replacement,' the old buyer said. 'Or, better still, get a date in her diary for you to meet her. The other suppliers are already queuing up, so you'll be ahead of the curve.'

'Oh, don't worry about me,' the Bold Businessman said dismissively. 'I'll get there sooner or later. Besides, your store already knows us very well and has been happily buying our products for years.'

The old buyer frowned, but didn't say anything.

Eventually, it was the New Buyer herself who called to make an appointment to meet the Bold Businessman. She'd waited long enough.

The Bold Businessman decided he would impress his new client and show her how important he was. He hired a helicopter to take him to the meeting.

Rather than be impressed with the man's success, the New Buyer thought the Bold Businessman was showy and arrogant. He was clearly making far too much money if he could afford to travel everywhere in a helicopter.

The New Buyer decided she either needed much lower prices, or one of the other suppliers would get the business.

Nurture each new relationship as though it
was your first. Past glories count for little.

THE KIND-HEARTED SHOPKEEPER AND THE THREE BROTHERS

The Kind-Hearted Shopkeeper had known the Three Brothers for many years. They had grown up together in the same town.

One day, the eldest of the three brothers went to see the Kind-Hearted Shopkeeper to ask for his advice and help. He and his brothers had made an interesting new dessert at their kitchen table, which they felt sure would sell well. The trouble was, they weren't sure if they should give up their well-paid jobs and risk starting a small food manufacturing business.

The Kind-Hearted Shopkeeper tried the dessert and was very encouraging.

'If you start this business, I will stock these in my shops,' he promised, 'and pay you promptly.'

The eldest brother was very grateful.

'We will give you a good price as our first ever customer,' he said. 'Thank you so much.'

Buoyed by the Kind-Hearted Shopkeeper's words, the Three Brothers set up their Hot Cakes business. Sure enough, it was a huge success. The Kind-Hearted Shopkeeper stuck to his word and bought the desserts from the brothers and was happy to see many more shops follow his lead.

It was not until many years later that the Kind-Hearted Shopkeeper was horrified to discover that the Three Brothers were giving his rivals far better discounts and agreeing to take much later payment. Even far smaller businesses were getting discounts substantially lower than he was.

While the Kind-Hearted Shopkeeper's generosity had helped start the business, the Three Brothers had not thought twice about buying the business of others at his expense.

Kindness of heart is commendable,
but not if it puts your business and your
people at a disadvantage.

THE DILIGENT MANAGING DIRECTOR'S VISITS

The Diligent Managing Director of Stayover spent one day a week visiting the hotels in his large chain. His PA would efficiently set out a schedule of visits and allocate time with the manager in each one. The Diligent Managing Director was also sure to randomly visit one of his competitors' hotels while he was in the area.

Each week the Diligent Managing Director would marvel at how much better Stayover hotels looked and functioned than those of its rivals. This, he believed, spoke volumes about his leadership and that of his management team.

The Diligent Managing Director was, however, a little mystified that independent industry surveys repeatedly ranked other hotel groups above his own. And why were rival groups winning so many awards, when Stayover's medal cabinet stayed empty? *It must be a conspiracy*, he thought.

One day, the Diligent Managing Director's PA took time off sick. This meant no one was able to notify Stayover hotels of the Diligent Managing Director's impending visit. Sure enough, the Diligent Managing Director found that he

Stayover hotels he saw that week were nowhere near as good as those of his competitors.

The Diligent Managing Director resolved to carry out more unannounced visits in the future.

Always try to see your business
as your customers do.

THE SELF-IMPORTANT
CHIEF EXECUTIVE'S LUNCHES

The Self-Important Chief Executive ruled his food business with an iron fist. Each week he would hold a lunch where he would taste all the new products. Buyers, product developers and chefs would tremble as the Self-Important Chief Executive would scream out his verdict.

'More salt, more sugar, more pepper,' he'd explode, among a million other complaints.

The government then brought in rules to reduce the amount of salt and sugar in products.

'Rubbish,' boomed the Self-Important Chief Executive. 'I'll decide what is right for our food. I am not pandering to the nanny state!'

His product developers felt differently, but were too afraid to say anything.

Then the government required that labels were put on packs to show how much sugar and salt were in products.

'Rubbish,' roared the Self-Important Chief Executive. 'I know what I like. We are not following the guidance.'

His buyers didn't agree, but stayed quiet because they

were scared of him.

Then the government brought in new guidance on portion sizes.

'Rubbish,' bayed the Self-Important Chief Executive. 'It is for our customers to decide how much they eat.'

His team of nutritionists did not believe this to be true, but said nothing.

Soon, the talented and experienced team began to leave to find somewhere that their voices would be heard. Eventually customers went elsewhere too, because they were not being given what *they* wanted.

> *Having many views and ideas expressed*
> *is better than only having one. Failure awaits*
> *if you do not nurture diversity.*

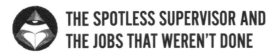

THE SPOTLESS SUPERVISOR AND THE JOBS THAT WEREN'T DONE

The Managing Director of Trim was worried about one of the hair salons in his chain. While all of the other hundred or more salons were doing brilliantly, this one seemed to be permanently in the doldrums.

She decided to pay a visit to the struggling salon and walked the floor with the Spotless Supervisor.

The Managing Director immediately noticed an opportunity to add an extra sales fixture at the front of the shop and pointed out where it could go.

'I have long wanted to do that,' agreed the Spotless Supervisor. 'But I can't get the money I need from the Area Manager.'

The Managing Director then noticed a glut of one particular type of shampoo on the shelf.

'I know,' said the Spotless Supervisor with an exasperated shrug. 'I have asked the buyer for markdown money to get rid of it but they say there is none.'

The Managing Director turned to see a number of spotlights that were not working and pointed them out.

'I can't tell you how long I have been waiting for the maintenance department to fix them,' said the Spotless Supervisor.

'But you are managing this shop, you must take control,' said the Managing Director. 'Your success rests in your ability to get things done.'

'But I am doing my best!' replied the Spotless Supervisor.

'That is just what I was afraid of – you're fired!' said the Managing Director.

The best will find a way.

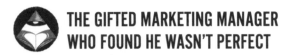

THE GIFTED MARKETING MANAGER WHO FOUND HE WASN'T PERFECT

Everybody knew the Gifted Marketing Manager was a very creative individual and had oodles of great ideas. However, when it came to getting stuff done, it often just didn't happen. Yet no one was a tougher critic of his work than the Gifted Marketing Manager himself. He was a complete perfectionist, but the truth was he wasn't very good at the detail and wasn't much of a people person either.

The Gifted Marketing Manager was becoming more and more frustrated because he felt a lot of his brilliant ideas were going to waste, as either they didn't get traction or failed due to a lack of proper planning.

The Gifted Marketing Manager's wise boss understood his skills and deficiencies. He took the Gifted Marketing Manager aside and explained to him that there were things he was utterly brilliant at, but there were other things he was less good at doing.

'Just focus on the things you do wonderfully well, because no one is better,' said the wise boss.

At first the Gifted Marketing Manager was sceptical, but

he was reassured by his boss. The senior man brought in a new team to help the Gifted Marketing Manager do the things he disliked really well. He recruited someone with brilliant people skills who kept the team positive and united. Another loved going through the detail of the work and would rejoice in making things just perfect. Yet another was motivated by making things happen and got the greatest pleasure from completing a project on time and to budget. Everyone enjoyed their roles and the team was very successful.

Nobody is perfect, but a team can be.

THE LOYAL CUSTOMER AND THE COSTLY TEA BAG

Like clockwork, the Loyal Customer would visit the same cafe at 11 o'clock every day and ask for their usual green tea. But on this particular day, the waitress explained that there was a promotion and they were only selling lemon green tea for that week.

'But I don't want lemon in my green tea, I just want green tea,' explained the Loyal Customer.

'I'm sorry, but I have been told we can only sell the teas on promotion,' explained the waitress. 'We have done a deal with the company.'

'Why can't you just go and get a box of green tea from the shelf over there?' asked the Loyal Customer.

'I don't have permission to do that, we have to sell these lines on promotion,' insisted the waitress, feeling a little exasperated.

'What if I told you I was allergic to lemon?' asked the Loyal Customer.

'I still can't serve you your usual green tea,' said the waitress. 'I'm not allowed.'

'In that case, I will go elsewhere for my green tea,' said the Loyal Customer defiantly and never returned to the cafe again.

It is futile to argue over a teabag.
A loyal customer's future business
is worth more.

CHAPTER FOUR

Attitude – A little thing that makes a big difference

THE PROUD MANAGER AND HIS CORNER OFFICE

The Proud Manager loved his corner office at the engineering firm where he had worked since his apprenticeship. After years of hard work at Plugged In, he'd finally moved into the coveted spot and felt it rightly reflected his achievements.

He didn't consider he was showing off at all when he insisted that his junior colleagues always came to the sumptuous, richly furnished corner office for meetings. After all, he reasoned, he was more important and his time far more precious.

The Proud Manager was a little surprised that the Plugged In boss was always willing to visit his corner office for meetings too. However, that didn't stop him boasting about it to his colleagues.

'Perhaps I am destined for an even better office,' the Proud Manager declared. 'Did you know I am the only person on this floor who *always* hosts the boss.'

'That is very interesting,' replied a wise colleague quietly. 'Tell me, when do the meetings begin?'

'When the boss arrives,' said the Proud Manager.

'And end?'

'When the boss decides to leave,' said the Proud Manager slowly.

'And I am sure you are always more relaxed in your corner office and say exactly what is on your mind,' smiled the wise colleague.

'I'm sure the boss thinks you are both in entirely the right place.'

There is real power in humility.

THE SCEPTICAL SHOPKEEPER
AND THE BIRD SEED

It was a glorious hot summer and sales of cold drinks were going through the roof at the Kitchen Sink pound store. The Sceptical Shopkeeper couldn't believe her eyes when she saw a memo from head office.

'Please re-stock the promotional fixtures with bird seed,' it read.

'What?' the Sceptical Shopkeeper exclaimed, reading the memo again. 'That can't be right. Surely they can't expect me to take down all these refreshing drinks from the promotional rack. We are in the middle of a heat wave.

'What idiots they are, sending their messages from their ivory towers. They need to open a window now and again.'

That afternoon a large delivery of bird seed arrived. The Sceptical Shopkeeper refused to give it space in her stock room; she sent it all straight back to head office.

When she got home that evening, the Sceptical Shopkeeper switched on the TV news.

The headline announcement blared out:

'Households are being urged to stock-up on birdseed. Conser-

vationists have announced that millions of birds are dying in the current heat wave. A combination of failed crops, hardened soil and an explosion of pests is threatening an environmental catastrophe.'

The following morning shoppers flocked to the Kitchen Sink store to help do their bit. The Sceptical Shopkeeper could only offer them cold drinks.

Find out the reason for someone's
actions before you react.

THE OVERBEARING MANAGER AND THE EXTENSION

Everybody was afraid of the Overbearing Manager, but the bosses at Swell Inc. loved him. They knew that when he told the factory staff to jump, the response would always come back: 'How high?'.

When Swell Inc. ran into a spot of bother with a landowner playing hardball, the Overbearing Manager seemed the obvious choice to send over to sort the situation out.

'We need to buy his land to extend the factory, but he doesn't seem interested in selling to us,' they told the Overbearing Manager. 'Sort it out and there is a promotion in it for you.'

'No problem,' said the Overbearing Manager.

This will be easy, he thought.

The Overbearing Manager went to see the landowner and told him that a deal needed to be done right away.

'I'm really sorry, but I am already talking to someone else,' replied the landowner politely.

'Listen,' said the Overbearing Manager menacingly. 'Swell Inc. is a big business and the largest local employer. Ours is the best offer you're going to get. You should sell to us now. If you don't, it will look very bad for you.'

The landowner didn't like being bullied and said he would like to deal with his original buyer.

'But you *have* to sell to me,' shouted the Overbearing Manager, unable to control his fury at the snub.

'Nobody *has* to do anything,' said the landowner calmly.

The landowner signed a deal with someone else and the Overbearing Manager didn't get his promotion.

> *Persuading people is a very different skill from*
> *telling people. If there is no obligation to act,*
> *no amount of bullying will work.*

THE FRETTING MANAGER
AND THE REPORTS

It was all going wrong and the Fretting Manager didn't know why. He was spending more and more time in his office poring over report, after report, after report. Sales at Bite-Easy were down, wastage was up and the marketing budget was overspent.

On a surprise visit the Bite-Easy Area Manager was confused to find the store apparently with no manager and the staff listlessly sitting waiting for non-existent customers. He knocked at the Fretting Manager's office door and was worried to see his colleague slumped over paperwork.

'I can't see what's wrong,' said the Fretting Manager who was clearly troubled.

'Come with me,' said the Area Manager, opening the office door and leading the Fretting Manager out.

When the Fretting Manager reached the Bite-Easy shop floor he was horrified by what he saw. The fruit and vegetable fixtures were empty, while unsold meat was piled high in the chillers.

The Fretting Manager glanced over at the checkouts.

Each one was open, but there were barely any customers to serve.

'Now can you see what's wrong?' asked the Area Manager.

Live in the here and now. Pay attention to
what is happening today, rather than
relying on yesterday's report.

THE FOOTBALL FAN
AND THE SUPPLIER

The Football Fan could hardly contain his excitement when one of his suppliers visited his office and offered him tickets to the Cup Final. He had supported the same team for decades and this year was their big opportunity to win the cup.

The supplier, of course, saw this as a great opportunity to worm his way into the Football Fan's favour.

The big day came and the Football Fan had a great time. His team won and the supplier didn't scrimp on the hospitality.

The following season, the Football Fan's team got to the Cup Final once again. Rather cheekily, he called the supplier and asked if he could help him out again.

The supplier explained that he had already promised the tickets they had to someone else. However, he did say he could help the Football Fan get tickets since he had some good contacts.

The Football Fan was overjoyed and asked for five tickets so he could take his whole family. The tickets arrived and the buyer and his family enjoyed a wonderful day. They had a marvellous lunch, amazing seats next to the Royal Box and his team won 2–0. Things couldn't get better. The Football Fan wrote and thanked the supplier for his kindness.

Two weeks later, the Football Fan received a copy of an invoice for the Cup Final hospitality package. The supplier requested payment in thirty days. It had cost £10,000! The Football Fan called the supplier and explained that he thought the tickets were free, just as before. He simply couldn't afford to pay that much.

After a pause the wily old supplier said the Football Fan could 'owe him'. He then deftly turned the conversation to a negotiation on pricing.

> *Never put yourself in a position where you*
> *feel morally indebted. It will cost you more*
> *than you'd ever imagine.*

THE ORGANISED FACTORY MANAGER AND THE VIP VISIT

There was a big hoo-hah at the Indulgent chocolate factory, since they were shortly expecting a very important visitor.

'The VIP will be here at the end of the week, so I must get all my orders done, my production line spotless and staff trained,' said the Organised Factory Manager. She began to make many lists and to tick tasks off as she completed them.

'Relax,' soothed her colleague, the Laid-Back Manager. 'There is loads of time to do all that. The visit isn't for ages. We can have a few easy days then put our foot down on Wednesday.'

So, the Organised Factory Manager beavered on whilst the Laid-Back Manager watched. The Laid-Back Manager had a relaxing week, putting all his important tasks off and enjoying feeling superior to the frantically busy Organised Factory Manager.

But, on Wednesday, there was a flood in the Indulgent building and as a result everyone needed to help out. The Laid-Back Manager began to panic because he wasn't able to get on with the things he needed to do before the VIP's visit.

When the VIP arrived the next day, the Laid-Back Manager was keen to blame the flood for his lack of preparation. But the VIP could see that the Organised Factory Manager had completed all her tasks regardless.

If it needs doing – do it now.

THE LETHARGIC WORKER
AND THE FOOTBALL STAR

The boss of Ownco noticed that one of her most successful team members had been less energetic and interested recently, resting on the laurels of past successes. It concerned her greatly, since the large property company liked everyone to be constantly at the top of their game impressing prospective clients. She asked the Lethargic Worker to come to see her and, when he arrived, was shocked by how relaxed and uninterested he appeared.

The Ownco boss knew that the Lethargic Worker was a big football fan, so she chose her words carefully.

'Christiano Ronaldo has on several occasions been voted the best player in the world,' she began. 'He has tremendous natural ability, physical presence, balance and mental strength. He's good enough to waltz into most teams.

'But I am told that both at Manchester United and Real Madrid he was the hardest working player in training and would spend many extra hours practising his free kicks so that he would become the world's greatest. For him being selected by Manchester United and then Real Madrid was the start, not the finish!'

The Lethargic Worker immediately saw the point, and redoubled his effort.

Continued and sustained success
requires hard work and dedication.
Always.

THE CYNICAL EXECUTIVE AND THE ANNUAL PERFORMANCE REVIEW

The Cynical Executive always hated the rigmarole of the annual performance review.

'It doesn't matter which company I work for, the routine is the same,' she complained to her new colleague at Quench. 'My boss will tell me all the things I am doing wrong and then give me a "to do" list for the year ahead. It's a complete waste of time.'

'It's different here.' Her colleague smiled.

And it was. At the review the Cynical Executive was asked how she had settled in and what had been her greatest successes, and the manager appeared genuinely interested in the answer. The Cynical Executive was asked if she had what she needed to do her job to the best of her ability. When she mentioned a few things that might help, the manager assured her they'd be sorted.

It was a breath of fresh air for the Cynical Executive to have her successes celebrated and frustrations explored.

At the end of the annual performance review the Quench manager asked the Cynical Executive what three objectives she wanted to achieve that year and what help he could give. The manager also mentioned one thing in passing that he would really appreciate her help in solving. The Cynical Executive willingly agreed.

The review letter that followed set the same positive frame. The Cynical Executive felt good and excelled.

It is liberating to achieve your own objectives.
It is slavery to complete someone else's.

THE IMPATIENT CHIEF EXECUTIVE AND THE TRACTOR

The Impatient Chief Executive was being driven to visit an under-performing business. He was very frustrated to be held up by a tractor on the road ahead. The long queue of cars behind it and the windy roads made it impossible to overtake.

'I'm going to be late,' the Impatient Chief Executive growled to his driver. 'Why didn't you take the faster motorway route?'

'I'm sorry, sir, I thought this way would be more scenic. I can't go any faster,' the driver replied.

The Impatient Chief Executive finally arrived at his destination and started his individual meetings with the department heads. He asked each one why they hadn't done this, that and the other to make the business better. One after another they replied that they had sent requests for funding to improve things to the Finance Director ages ago, but were still waiting for a reply. The Impatient Chief Executive went to see the Finance Director. Across a desk pulled high with papers the Finance Director argued that it took time to make these decisions; there was only so much money and more information was required.

As he drove back to the office, on clear roads this time, the Impatient Chief Executive pondered on the issue. Thanks to the time the Finance Director was taking to make a decision, his business was grinding to a halt. It occurred to him the situation in this under-performing division was very similar to his journey that morning. He phoned the Finance Director on his return and asked if he could speed up.

'I'm doing the best I can,' replied the finance man.

'That's exactly what I was afraid of, I'm afraid you're fired,' said the Impatient Chief Executive, ending the call.

On the road and in business you
can only go as fast as the slowest.

THE CONTENTED DEPARTMENT STORE MANAGER AND THE LAW OF AVERAGES

The Contented Department Store Manager was perfectly happy that his sales and service scores were ahead of the rest of the group's. He was therefore surprised to receive a visit from the Area Manager, who didn't seem to be blown away by his performance.

'But I have *consistently* high standards,' the Contented Department Store Manager crowed.

'Really?' asked the Area Manager. 'I wonder if you might take a walk with me.'

It was lunchtime when they got to the stationery department, which was very busy with customers who had dashed out of work to buy greetings cards. They were only on the shop floor for a few seconds before they heard customers complaining that they couldn't easily find the card they needed and were in a hurry. The queue at the till was massive as the cashier chatted to each customer about the occasion they had bought the card for. Toes were tapping in the queue and a number of customers were dumping their cards and walking out.

The Contented Department Store Manager looked a

little uncomfortable. Luckily the Area Manager ushered him towards the fashion department. There, knowledgeable staff were deftly helping customers put an outfit together, checking on them in the fitting rooms and lovingly wrapping their purchases. The customers looked very happy.

'You see how the components of good service are very different in the two departments?' the Area Manager explained. 'Whilst your sales may on average be above the group and your customer service scores high on average, you have huge inconsistencies. My measure of your ability as a manager is how narrow the gap is on all measures between the best and the worst performing departments.'

If you have your head in the oven and your
feet in the fridge you will have an average
body temperature.

THE EAGER MANAGER AND THE LOSS-MAKING CARPET FITTERS

The Rolls carpet-fitting business had been losing money for years and the Eager Manager was charged with turning it around. Keen to prove his worth, the Eager Manager travelled with the fitters day after day to see what could be done.

After a few days the Eager Manager noticed that the fitters always fitted aluminium door strips, separating the carpets in one room from another.

'Do we not stock other door strips?' he asked one of the carpet estimators.

'Yes, we stock brass ones too, but we always put aluminium on the estimate since it is by far the cheapest,' said the experienced estimator.

'What do each cost?' asked the Eager Manager.

'The aluminium strips cost us £1.50 and we sell them for £1.60 as that is what they cost elsewhere,' he explained. 'The brass strips cost us £3 and we sell them for £6.'

'From now on I want you to estimate for brass, then if the customer thinks the overall cost too high there will be an easy way to reduce it,' said the Eager Manager.

The Rolls losses started to shrink as few customers questioned the cost of the door strip.

Extra profit can be built with
the smallest changes.

THE CANNY MANAGER AND SOMETHING FOR NOTHING

The Canny Manager travelled with the Big White electrical retailers delivery team regularly to see if he could spot any improvements that could be made. He realised that the drivers were spending a lot of time removing old washing machines and fridges and disposing of them.

He instructed the sales team and drivers that Big White had a new policy. The business would no longer offer to take the customers' old fridges and washing machines away free of charge, but rather give them the number of the local council's refuse department to arrange a collection. Alternatively, Big White could dispose of them for the customer for a charge of £10 an appliance.

Most customers couldn't be bothered with the hassle of arranging a collection and so paid for removal. The business became very profitable and the Canny Manager was promoted.

Think creatively. There is always money
in the things no one seems to want

CHAPTER FIVE

Engaging Customers –
Where the story begins

THE NAIVE NEW MD AND THE CUSTOMER-CENTRIC BUSINESS

For as long as anyone could remember, Shoptastic had been the biggest and best department store. People would travel from far and wide so that they could spend time at their nearest Shoptastic.

When a new management team took over at Shoptastic, they all knew to be very careful with the brand.

'Remember, the customer is always right,' warned the Naive New MD.

The new management team agreed upon a customer survey to see what Shoptastic customers wanted. The results were clear: whilst most customers were delighted with the shop, some said they would like a cafe.

The Naive New MD created some space for a new cafe.

Surprisingly, once the cafe opened, Shoptastic began to receive complaints.

'What has happened to the kitchen equipment you used to stock?' demanded the customers. 'Your new cafe has taken a bite out of the kitchen department.'

The Naive New MD knew the customer was always right

and so created more space for kitchen equipment by taking the space from the bathroom fixtures next door.

But the customers showered the staff with protests.

'We can't find the bathroom fittings we need,' they wailed.

The Naive New MD duly reinstated the bathroom fittings, shuffling the stationery department into a new, smaller space.

But now no one was happy and stationery sales ground to a halt. Alarmed, the Naive New MD closed the cafe and put everything back to the way things were.

'But where is our lovely new cafe?' the customers cried.

The customer is not always right.

THE CAR PARK ATTENDANT AND
THE CUSTOMER WITH TOOTHACHE

It was 23 December, the busiest shopping day of the year for the supermarket, and the Car Park Attendant was doing his best to direct traffic in and out of the small car park. There was quite a queue of cars but, on the whole, customers were being good humoured.

The Car Park Attendant was amazed when one shopper parked his car and then began to walk away in the opposite direction to the supermarket.

'Are you not shopping with us today, sir?' he asked politely.

'No, no. I have an urgent appointment at the dentist close by,' the chap explained.

'But, you can't park here to visit the dentist, we need all the spaces for our customers,' said the Car Park Attendant.

'But I *am* one of your customers,' said the man with toothache. 'I regularly shop with you and then do some bits and pieces elsewhere in the town.'

The Car Park Attendant took a deep breath.

'Yes, we normally give our customers an hour and a half free parking to do that, but because today is our busiest day of the year the spaces are solely for customers just shopping with us,' he explained calmly. 'Otherwise we disappoint those who want to shop here.'

'But I urgently need to get to the dentist!' protested the customer.

'Well, there are other pay-and -display car parks near by, or you can park in the street,' the Car Park Attendant suggested.

The customer drove away feeling very cross and never visited the shop again.

> *Even if you know they are wrong,*
> *the customer is judge and jury.*

THE STUDIOUS SHOPKEEPER AND THE GOLDEN JUBILEE

It was the build-up to the Queen's Golden Jubilee and the Studious Shopkeeper at a branch of Fabrication, a large cloth business, had just received a message from central office. It was from the new boss telling her where to place coloured fabrics so as to improve sales. It was the first time she had *ever* received such instruction.

After day one of the promotion, blue fabrics had sold out, but instead of using her initiative and remerchandising as she would normally do, the Studious Shopkeeper went back to check in with head office. The next day a white roll sold out and she called head office again. The phones in head office were soon red hot with queries about what should be restocked and what should be put where. Studious Shopkeepers from all over the Fabrication store network were confused.

'My goodness, it is worse than we feared,' said the Fabrication boss in a panic. 'My shopkeepers need so much help. I must get more staff.'

Soon there were hundreds of people in central office employed to tell experienced shop managers precisely what to do, writing new central procedures for *everything* and answering branch helplines. The Studious Shopkeeper and her colleagues quickly found they enjoyed their jobs less and less.

As word got out, fewer people wanted to work at the company and profits were cut to ribbons.

Think very carefully about removing accountability
and responsibility from those who come into contact
with the customer daily.

THE YOUNG ENTREPRENEUR
AND THE CHAMPAGNE

Everybody admired the Young Entrepreneur who had taken on all of his bigger, established rivals by selling cut-priced wines. He felt very pleased with himself too, because he had managed to build a chain of more than two dozen of his Uncorked shops.

At Christmas, the Young Entrepreneur had a great idea: he'd sell cut-price champagne and then even more people would flock to his shops.

Unfortunately, the Young Entrepreneur had a problem. The top champagne producers refused to sell to him. They didn't want to devalue their finest products.

'Never mind, I'll do exactly what's worked like a charm for me before,' said the Young Entrepreneur. 'I'll buy just one case from elsewhere and advertise that I'll sell the champagne at ridiculously low prices and everyone will be talking about Uncorked.'

Sure enough, everyone went wild about top-class champagne being sold for just twenty pounds when the press printed huge stories declaring it *the* bargain of the festive season.

Uncorked sold out of its one case of fine discounted

champagne in under an hour and the many, many customers who ran to the shops fizzing in excitement were sorely disappointed.

'We've been conned,' they cried. 'We'll shop elsewhere in future.'

You can only fool people for so long.

THE PERFECT BREADMAKER'S BAKERY

The Perfect Breadmaker worked hard to make her Bread Basket bakery successful. She bought good-quality flour to make good-quality bread, mixed and kneaded it for just the right amount of time and baked it in an oven at exactly the right temperature and for the exact right amount of time. The prized loaves were sold in her clean and neat shop, where they were laid out in perfect symmetry and could be bought for just a few pennies. Over the years, the Perfect Breadmaker built up a happy and loyal following.

Eventually, the Perfect Breadmaker grew old. The early morning starts, seven days a week, fifty-two weeks a year, made her feel constantly tired. Her muscles ached from kneading the dough. She was reluctant to retire, but felt happy that she was handing the Bread Basket business over to her highly educated and well-travelled son.

The Perfect Breadmaker's son was very excited. He'd waited years to take over the business and had ambitious plans for it. He wanted to sell patisserie, viennoiserie and the finest pastries to attract more customers. He recruited one of the top pastry chefs and spent lots of money lavishly decorating the Perfect Breadmaker's shop. He even renamed the shop The Flaky Croissant.

The day The Flaky Croissant shop reopened, the Perfect Breadmaker's son was aghast. He saw the regular customers stop, look in the window and then carry on about their business without stepping inside. Worse still, later in the morning, he saw them walking by clutching loaves from a rival baker. They wanted the familiar taste of plain bread at a price they could afford.

'What is wrong with them?' the Perfect Breadmaker's son stormed. 'Why can't they see this is a cut above?'

The Perfect Breadmaker herself was silent.

Keep things simple.
Know what your customers want.

THE BORED ASSISTANT ON THE NEW DOOR

The Luxanova jewellery business spent thousands buying the new shop and thousands more refurbishing it. The store looked fantastic. The gold-embossed doors twinkled, the glass shelves were polished to a high shine and the floor was covered in luxurious thick-pile carpets. The display units were the best that money could buy.

Staff from Luxanova's old store were all moved to the new one and most of them were delighted with what they found. All, that is, except for the Bored Assistant, who found it all rather dull.

On the great day of the store opening, Luxanova's boss asked the Bored Assistant to hand out leaflets at the entrance. She figured this might help the Bored Assistant to feel involved.

Perhaps if he sees the excitement of all our customers, he will become enthusiastic too, she thought.

When the doors opened, customers flooded in to see what all the fuss was about. The Luxanova boss stood behind the tills smiling and waiting to ask customers what they thought. She expected mountains of praise.

'Do you like the new shop?' she asked a couple as they left.

'Not really,' came the reply. 'The staff member handing out leaflets on the door looked glum and uninterested. He didn't return our smile and, when we asked for directions, he couldn't be bothered to answer. It put us off from the start.'

You never get a second chance
to make a first impression.

THE CONCEITED CHAIRMAN AND THE BAD PAPER

There were once two paper companies, Jotize and Padso. Jotize was a new business, which wasn't a significant size yet, but it had big plans. Its unique selling point was that all its paper was ethically and sustainably sourced and part of its profits went towards helping troubled communities where the timber came from. Padso was the established company in the sector, which had been around for years and had grown to be very large indeed.

The Conceited Chairman of Padso wasn't happy about Jotize. He didn't like competition.

'We will wipe them out,' crowed the Conceited Chairman. 'Customers love low prices.'

Under orders from Padso's Conceited Chairman, its buyers scoured the world to find the cheapest paper possible. Triumphantly, they bought it all up and raced to get it into the shops.

To drive the message home, the Conceited Chairman spent a fortune on a marketing campaign to tell everyone what a fantastic bargain Padso's paper was.

He was right, customers love a bargain. Everyone shopped at Padso and Jotize began to suffer.

Then, one day, a clever journalist did some digging. After all the fuss about Padso, they wanted to know how the company managed to sell its paper so cheaply. He discovered Padso could sell for less because it had terrible ethical values. Its paper was illegally sourced from forests that were not sustainably managed. The producers used child labour and dangerous chemicals in their paper production too. Customers were horrified. They flocked to Jotize and bought its paper even though it cost a little more.

Cheap is not always best. Don't underestimate or ignore your customers' values.

THE PERSISTENT MANAGER AND THE DISSATISFIED CUSTOMER

The Dissatisfied Customer arrived at the grocery store and asked to speak to the manager right away.

'I bought a meal from the shop last week and became very unwell,' he complained.

'That is awful, do you have the product?' asked the Persistent Manager. 'That way we can test to see if it was at fault.'

'No, I ate it a week ago,' said the Dissatisfied Customer.

'Do you have a sample?' pressed the Persistent Manager. 'If we test that we can tell what caused your upset stomach?'

'What! No, don't be silly,' replied the Dissatisfied Customer, getting agitated.

'Well, do you have the packaging?' asked the Persistent Manager. 'The information on that can tell us if there was a fault with your batch of products.'

'No!' replied the Dissatisfied Customer sharply.

'Well, do you have your receipt? That will give me the date of purchase and I can see if there were any other reports of illness from similar products bought on that day.' continued the Persistent Manager.

'It's quite clear you don't trust me,' stormed the Dissatisfied Customer. 'I'm not going to shop here again.'

And the customer left promising never to return.

Process should never get in the way of
dealing with a customer's concerns.

THE COMPLAINING CUSTOMER AND THE FAULTY TYRE

There was once a department store that was famed for its customer service. One day, everyone on the shop floor was surprised to see a customer walk in carrying a car tyre. He strode to the service desk and explained that he had purchased the tyre at that store, discovered it was faulty and would now like a full refund.

'But we don't sell tyres,' said the Customer Services Assistant, looking bemused.

'You do,' insisted the Complaining Customer. 'I know that, because I bought this tyre from here.'

'Might it not have perhaps been from the shop just down the road?' said the Customer Services Assistant helpfully. 'They have an automotive department and sell tyres.'

'I know where I bought this tyre from,' exploded the Complaining Customer. 'I am one of your best customers.'

'How much did you pay sir?' asked the Customer Services Assistant.

'One hundred pounds,' said the Complaining Customer.

The Customer Services Assistant then credited the

Complaining Customer's card with one hundred pounds for the tyre and a further ten for the inconvenience of bringing it back, even though she knew the shop had never sold tyres.

The Complaining Customer went away happy.

Even if a customer is wrong, it is better to spend a little to keep them happy. If you don't, you may lose their business for good.

THE PRUDENT MANAGING DIRECTOR AND THE REWARD FOR LOYALTY

The Prudent Managing Director was thinking hard about how to improve sales at his supermarket and called in his Marketing Director for a chat.

'How many customers do we serve each year?' the Prudent Managing Director asked the Marketing Director.

'About ten million,' his colleague replied.

'Of those, how many are the most loyal?' asked the Prudent Managing Director. 'By that I mean, shop with us week after week?'

'Oh, about a tenth,' said the Marketing Director. 'Although those million do punch above their weight. They generate about 50 per cent of our trade.'

'So why do we spend our entire marketing budget on attracting new customers, who we know don't stick around, or spend money, for long?' asked the Prudent Managing Director. 'Meanwhile, we don't spend a penny on our best customers.'

The Prudent Managing Director immediately shifted all his advertising and marketing spend to invest in his loyal customers and added a reward if they got their friends to shop with the company too.

> *Value the customers you have. Word of mouth is the most powerful advertising.*

THE INDIGNANT CASHIER
AND THE COMPLAINTS

Ring, ring, went the bell above the till of Cash Desk number four. The Grocery Store Manager hurried over.

'This customer says she bought some apples and they didn't last long before she had to throw them out,' said the Indignant Cashier. 'Now she wants a refund.'

'Of course,' said the Grocery Store Manager. 'Please give her her money back and a voucher to spend next time for her inconvenience.'

Ring, ring, went the bell above the till of Cash Desk number four. The Grocery Store Manager hurried over.

'This man has brought back some wine and reckons it is corked,' growled the Indignant Cashier. 'There is only a bit left in the bottle and he bought it months ago.'

It was clear the Indignant Cashier fully expected the Grocery Store Manager to bat away the complaint.

'That's fine, replace it and give this gentleman another bottle for free,' said the Grocery Store Manager to the Indignant Cashier's total disbelief.

Ring, ring, went the bell above the till of Cash Desk number four. The Grocery Store Manager hurried over.

'This customer says she didn't like the ready meal she bought,' said the Indignant Cashier, fixing the Grocery Store Manager with a steely stare. 'She has no receipt or anything.'

'Oh, I am sorry, please go and pick something else and take it away to try for free,' said the Grocery Store Manager to the customer. The Indignant Cashier shook her head.

When the ready meal customer had disappeared to find a new meal, the Indignant Cashier turned to the Grocery Store Manager. She could take it no more. 'Why are you being so generous to these complaining customers?' demanded the Indignant Cashier. 'I know we have a great reputation for customer service but in my old company they would have been shown the door. I think we are just wasting money.'

The Grocery Store Manager smiled and explained: 'It might seem generous but each of these people spend a lot of money with us each year. The cost of satisfying them is small compared to the millions we take and I have always found word-of-mouth advertising the cheapest and most profitable!'

*Consider the lifetime value of a
customer, not the immediate cost.*

THE KIND CAFE OWNER
AND THE BABY CHANGING ROOM

There was once a thriving cafe called Busy Bean, which everyone loved. Customers said they couldn't get enough of Busy Bean's home-made cakes and its coffee was divine.

'If there is one problem at all,' said a few, 'it is that Busy Bean needs a baby changing room.'

After many years of hearing this, the Kind Cafe Owner decided to do something about it. It wasn't easy, since the home of Busy Bean was old and small, but the Kind Cafe Owner found a little space at the back of the building. But much to her surprise she received more complaints than before.

'It's a little cramped,' a customer said.

'And very dark,' said another.

'Too cold,' complained another.

To the Kind Owner's surprise she had more disgruntled customers than before.

If you can't match customers'
expectations, it's better to do without.

CHAPTER SIX

Engaging the workforce

THE DEMORALISED HUMAN RESOURCES MANAGER AND THE GOOD FOOD

The Demoralised Human Resources Manager had had enough. Her firm was not doing very well and every time she took time and trouble to recruit a new worker, chances were they'd up and leave the moment they'd finished their training.

'It's not my fault they leave, we can't pay them enough,' she complained to the Managing Director. 'We could only afford to pay them more if productivity improves but without the training being given a chance to pay off, nothing ever moves on.'

The Managing Director listened quietly.

'Hmmm, it does seem a bit of a chicken and egg situation,' he agreed.

Then he had an idea.

'How about if we offer the best lunchtime food of any business and a first-rate staff restaurant with good amenities?' he suggested. 'That won't cost us very much and that way if people do leave, they should regret it every mealtime. And we can offer pedicures and hairdressing too, so that the staff feel well looked after.'

It worked! At last the well-trained staff stayed long enough to give the company that had invested in them the benefit. And as the company profits improved, they were paid more too!

Look after your people and they
will repay the business.

THE DELIVERY DRIVER
WHO WENT IT ALONE

The Delivery Driver had been working for the company for fifteen years and always did a good job. Then, one day, her bosses announced that, due to falling profits, all the drivers were to be made redundant and their work outsourced. The Delivery Driver and her colleagues were shattered.

But, the Delivery Driver was resourceful. She asked her boss if she could be one of the new outsourced drivers if she got a van and started her own business. The boss agreed, so long as her prices were competitive.

The Delivery Driver used her redundancy money to buy a van. She loved her van. Whereas before the Delivery Driver would take her old company van to the car wash when she thought about it, now she would wash, polish and buff it twice a week. Previously she never looked under the bonnet, leaving that for the mechanics at the annual service but now she checked her oil, water and tyre pressure weekly. The Delivery Driver drove more efficiently, conserving fuel and her brakes, so her van lasted longer than the ones her old company replaced annually. As it was her business, the Delivery Driver worked when she needed, not nine to five. She also now prided herself on her own appearance as well as her vehicle's.

As a result, the Delivery Driver got busier and busier. Customers appreciated her attitude and, because of that and her flexible approach, her old company kept giving her more to do. She was soon much better off than she had been before.

When you own something, you care more.

THE FED-UP PROMOTIONS EXECUTIVE AND THE CHATTY MANAGER

There were once two friends who both worked at the same company in promotions, but for different departments. One of them felt content and fulfilled in their job but the other wasn't very happy.

'What do you think the problem is?' asked the Happy Promotions Executive.

'I think the biggest issue is I can't get a word in edgeways,' shrugged her friend.

She then related a story about what had happened that very morning.

The Fed-Up Promotions Executive had gone into the office to be told about a new project. Her Chatty Manager launched straight into it.

'Right, we have been asked to think of a promotion for Mother's Day and all departments are competing against each other,' the Chatty Manager had burbled on. 'Now gather around and I will tell you what I am thinking. This is a perfect chance for me to show the top bosses how good I am!'

The Chatty Manager droned on and on with one idea after

another, barely pausing for breath. Then she'd gone on to give detailed instructions of what she wanted each member of the team to do.

'The thing is, I am sure we'd have come up with far more creative ideas if we had all worked together,' concluded the Fed-Up Promotions Executive.

And she was right, the Happy Promotions Executive's department involved and praised their team members for its ideas, and had won the competition easily.

> *There is no end to what you can achieve*
> *if you don't mind who gets the credit.*

THE OPEN AND HONEST MANAGER AND THE QUESTION OF TRUST

The Open and Honest Manager was always up for a challenge, so when he was asked to go to manage the struggling auto-parts division of his car firm SpinOut Auto, he went along willingly.

'It'll be difficult,' warned the SpinOut Auto boss. 'The team have a reputation for being unhelpful.'

Sure enough, the Open and Honest Manager quickly found the auto-parts team prepared to do no more than their contracts required.

'Will you stay a bit later tonight to finish an order?' asked the Open and Honest Manager. 'I'll give you the time off in lieu. Trust me.'

'No, we did that for the last managers and they never ever gave the time back,' came the reply. 'We were always too busy!'

'Could you swap between sections to speed things up?' asked the Open and Honest Manager. 'I will make sure that is reflected in your pay. Trust me.'

'No, that is what the last managers said,' came the reply. 'So we moved around and cross trained, but we never got an increase.'

'Could you alter your holiday dates to accommodate a

large order we have just received?' asked the Open and Honest Manager. 'If you do, I will give you a few extra days off. Trust me.'

'No, when we did that in the past we didn't get extra days,' came the reply. 'In fact we had trouble even rebooking our original holiday time.'

The Open and Honest Manager saw the magnitude of his challenge but he had a plan!

When he overheard one of the team saying he had an aching tooth, he sent him straight to the dentist and didn't ask for the lost work hours to be repaid. When a team member told him his daughter was performing in the school play, he insisted the worker went along to watch, hours paid. And, if someone had difficulty picking up a child from school, or needed to run a quick errand, he would let them. Before long the SpinOut Auto workers saw that they could trust the Open and Honest Manager and much to everyone's satisfaction the culture improved.

> *You need to give before you can take.*
> *Culture is the sediment of past transactions.*
> *It takes time and patience to change.*

THE KIND BAKERY OWNER
AND THE BREAD DELIVERY DRIVER

The young Bread Delivery Driver never really expected to stay at the bakery for long. He didn't expect to be missed much when he left either.

Then, one day, whilst making deliveries, he had a terrible accident which left him with bad injuries to his back and legs. He fully expected to lose his job straight away, but to his surprise the Kind Bakery Owner said he would keep his job open while he recovered and still pay him.

The Bread Delivery Driver was amazed. He was even more amazed when the Kind Bakery Owner called to say he had arranged for him to have weekly physiotherapy at the local football club. The Kind Bakery Owner then picked up the Bread Delivery Driver from his terraced home, drove him to the football ground for his appointment, waited with him and delivered him home afterwards. The Kind Bakery Owner did this throughout his employee's recovery without a word of complaint.

The Kind Bakery Owner and the Bread Delivery Driver talked a lot about the bread business during their time together and when he was fit again the Bread Delivery Driver returned to work completely committed to the owner and the business. His colleagues could also see just how much the Kind Bakery Owner valued his employees.

The Bread Delivery Driver stayed with the bakery for his entire career and, eager to learn, he rose to be a most loyal senior manager.

No one cares how much you know,
until they know how much you care.

THE COST CUTTING CEO
AND THE FINE WINE

MacFace always held an annual conference for its senior managers. A large conference venue would be selected in Europe and managers were required to make their own travel arrangements to get there.

This year was no different, but with a new Cost Cutting CEO everyone was eager to impress. Determined to save every penny possible, one keen manager scoured the internet to find the cheapest way to travel. Instead of getting a direct flight, he opted to fly economy to Brussels, change there, then catch a bus for the final leg of the journey to the conference venue. It was a complicated route but, in total, he would save one hundred pounds.. And that is what he did. But, to his frustration, he missed the connection and arrived four hours late. He was very frazzled indeed.

At the gala dinner that night he sat on the Cost Cutting CEO's table and apologised for missing the entire afternoon session.

'Don't worry,' boomed the Cost Cutting CEO. 'I've organised some marvellous wine that will cheer you up!'

The Keen Manager couldn't help but glance at the wine list. There, at the bottom of the list was the wine. It was £100 a bottle.

Don't expect one thing of your
team then do the opposite yourself.

THE INTERESTED MANAGER AND THE EARTH'S CORE

Everyone liked the Interested Manager. He never spent any time in his office. Instead he spent his days on the Brimstone factory floor alongside his workers. He knew everyone by name, their strengths and weaknesses and even the names of their family members.

The Interested Manager always noticed when things went badly, but he never got angry. He'd simply raise it with the team and asked for ideas on how to do it better next time.

The Interested Manager's enthusiasm lit fires in the staff who loved having an interest being taken in them and their work. People felt happy going to him for advice and greatly admired his energy and drive. In fact, they felt energised. As a result, the business, the Interested Manager and his team were very successful.

Everyone was very sad when the time came for the Interested Manager to retire.

'Don't worry, I have told the New Manager everything about you,' the Interested Manager assured the team. 'He knows how things are done around here.'

Before he left, the final piece of advice he gave the New Manager was: 'If you don't care, nobody else will.'

The New Manager thought these were all very sterling words, but couldn't help thinking the Interested Manager should have paid more attention to the paperwork that was piled up in his office. He decided to attend to the paperwork first and get to know the team as time went on.

'There is plenty of time to do all that,' he said to himself.

There never was enough time though. The New Manager never did get to know the names of all his team, nor their strengths and weaknesses, and certainly not their family circumstances. He rarely appeared on the factory floor, so was far less good at noticing what went on and helping.

With little interest being taken in them or their actions, the staff began to grow lazy and bored.

> *A manager is like the earth's core. If it is not*
> *sufficiently 'hot', all life and activity will die.*

THE PALLY PATENT LAWYER AND THE POOR PERFORMER

Everyone liked the Pally Patent Lawyer at Payne & Fears, but they all felt he had one weakness. He always gave too much leeway to one man on the team who was a very poor performer. When people urged the Pally Patent Lawyer to let the Poor Performer go, or put him in an easier position elsewhere, he refused.

'He has been with the company since the beginning,' he'd say. 'He's given us years of good service. Doesn't that deserve some loyalty?'

Privately, the Pally Patent Lawyer was concerned. The Poor Performer had become a good friend, but he was getting slower and slower and it was affecting the productivity of the entire department. With the Payne & Fears bonus system based on its performance, the clamour for action was getting hard to ignore.

Still, the Pally Patent Lawyer stuck by his man. By now, it had come to the notice of the partners in Payne & Fears that there was something wrong at this Pally Patent Lawyer's department. Good people were going elsewhere and the Poor Performer was dragging revenues down ever further.

'Talk to him about moving department or retraining or retiring,' the partners instructed the Pally Patent Lawyer.

But still the Pally Patent Lawyer did nothing. He didn't want to hurt the Poor Performer's feelings.

In no time at all, the department became consistently the worst performer and the Pally Patent Lawyer was fired. The Poor Performer followed him out of the door soon afterwards.

Don't let kind intentions get in the way.
Failing to deal with a poor performer
lets the whole team down.

THE SAVVY SUPERVISOR AND THE GRAFFITI

The Fixature DIY store was a terrible place to work. No one liked it there – neither customers nor staff. The fixtures were a mess, there were products all over the floor and the till countertops were filthy.

Eventually, the bosses at Fixature head office sold the shop to a rival, Totally Hammered, concluding it was a hopeless case.

Totally Hammered sent a Savvy Supervisor to oversee improvements at the shop, upgrading everything to attract customers back and improve staff facilities.

Everyone was involved in restocking and retraining and everything was carried out to the Savvy Supervisor's satisfaction. He was very encouraged that things were going to be better from then on. Then, the night before the grand reopening, someone sprayed graffiti in the newly refurbished lavatories.

The following morning, the Savvy Supervisor addressed the Fixature staff. He explained that he had called in a local decorator who had repainted the lavatories overnight to make them look good as new.

'Going forward, all of us will get a share of profits that this store makes,' he announced. 'However, the cost of the graffiti cleanup will be deducted from our first payment, including mine.'

From that moment on the staff were engaged in the shop's success, sick absence and staff turnover fell and there were no further instances of vandalism. The shop went from strength to strength.

When the team directly benefits from success, they care a little more.

CHAPTER SEVEN

Developing the team

THE SHINY NEW EXECUTIVE AND THE RAPID PROMOTION

Everyone at Myopica was impressed by the Shiny New Executive's easy charm and smooth demeanour. *Public school, public service, and a stint in consultancy – just perfect for us,* thought the senior manager who recruited her. *We'll push her on and up quickly.* She joined to help out in the production department and quickly made friends. In a short space of time, an opening came up in the personnel department. *It's no risk,* thought the senior manager who recruited her. *They are a very experienced team. They will cover any shortcomings.*

And so the Shiny New Executive moved over to Human Resources and, once again, everyone warmed to her. She was always smiling, willing to help and bought her efficient team treats.

Not many months passed and the CEO role came up in Myopica.

'This is your time,' said the senior manager who recruited her. 'I'm sure you'll be a breath of fresh air.'

And so it passed that with few enemies, a charming demeanour and much promise, the Shiny New Executive became chief.

Not long afterwards, there was an economic downturn. It badly affected Myopica and the pressure was on in every department as the company struggled to stay afloat.

Untried and untested by such events, the Shiny New Executive just didn't seem to be able to rally the troops and froze. In fact, her smile had completely disappeared and she became distant and uncommunicative. Without sufficient practical experience in the business or in finance, the Shiny New Executive just kept asking for more information for yet more plans but couldn't turn ideas into actions. Unrest grew amongst the experienced staff and many left, only to be replaced by newcomers with little experience and wanting information for plans, but who spoke the Shiny New Manager's language and made her feel more comfortable. Things began to get much worse.

Do not promote in haste and without seeing
how someone performs under real pressure.

THE INDEPENDENT MANAGER AND THE AIRLINE

Two airlines decided it was time to refit their business-class cabins. Both appointed experienced managers to oversee the work.

In the first airline, the Independent Manager relished being in charge of a project. She was very experienced and knew exactly what was wanted. The Independent Manager drew up a list of people to work with that she liked and trusted because she had worked with them before. When they met she gave them clear instructions about exactly what she wanted, leaving nothing out, whether it was the colour scheme of the seats, or the uniforms of the staff, or even the typeface for the menus. The contractors carefully followed her instructions and the refit was finished on time and on budget. The Independent Manager waited for the applause. But, to her surprise, there were grumbles all round. People said that the new design was 'OK' but not perfect!

The Thoughtful Manager in the second airline took her time to ponder on how to go about the task. She invited cabin crew to join her group to ask them what they thought customers would like in business-class. She did the same with the caterers, baggage handlers, check-in staff and frequent customers. The process was time consuming and, at times frustrating, as different people often had different ideas. Eventually though, with careful consideration, the Thoughtful Manager managed to come up with a design she believed everyone would love.

The second airline finished its refit some weeks after the first, but everyone inevitably compared it. It was declared that their design won hands down.

Even when you know what you
want it is worth consulting others.

THE STAR PLAYER
AND THE FASHION FIRM

There was no one at the clothing giant Fashionista who didn't know about the Star Player in the team. Even if they didn't, the Star Player himself would have quickly told them so. He dominated the entire company he was so confident and forthright. The Star Player always had brilliant ideas, gave marvellous speeches and was the life and soul of any gathering.

Whilst the Star Player's colleagues worked very hard, he never acknowledged their efforts. If he noted their contribution at all, it was to comment on how he was the root cause of their successes. The Star Player would delight in telling others that he was the main reason for their bonuses.

Bit by bit the Star Player's colleagues began to resent his swagger and poise. They became less interested in or committed to supporting his projects even though they knew they were often good ideas.

The owner of Fashionista decided things had gone too far. Taking the Star Player to one side she gently suggested he might like to recognise the efforts of his colleagues more often.

'After all, they provide the platform for you to do so well,' she said.

'Oh, nonsense,' said the Star Player. 'I'm afraid the team are all pretty average. Without me to raise them up, the entire firm would suffer. You are lucky to have me.'

The Fashionista boss didn't agree. In fact, she decided the firm would be all the better without the Star Player and let him go – and Fashionista continued to thrive.

A star player, and a business, can only perform
with the whole hearted support and commitment
of the entire team.

THE RELUCTANT MARKETER AND THE PROMOTION

The Chairman of Greens, the large department store, decided that after years of good growth, it was time to take the business to the next stage of development. He thought about it long and hard and decided what the store really needed was a clever marketing director.

All he had to do now was find the right man for the job.

As a rule, Greens always preferred to fill roles from within. Unfortunately, there was no obvious candidate. Greens had never employed a senior marketing person before. It didn't even have a marketing department.

The chairman looked around the company and made a choice, offering the new job of marketing director to a smart general manager.

'But why me?' asked the smart general manager. He had spent his whole career in operations and had never dreamed of working in marketing. 'Surely you want someone with experience of marketing?' protested the Reluctant Marketer.

He had spent his whole career in operations and had never dreamed of working in marketing.

The chairman explained that he could appoint an experienced marketer from outside the company who had relevant experience. However, an outsider would have absolutely no knowledge of the company's culture, or customers, which were very different from anything else on the High Street. Alternatively, the chairman could take a bright internal candidate who perfectly understood those things and could be trained in marketing.

The Reluctant Marketer accepted the job and the company trained him at the finest business schools. He quickly became a very effective marketer, combining his technical training with his business experience.

*Internal development and promotion should
be a company's first option. It will pay handsome dividends.*

THE SHARP SALES DIRECTOR AND HER WARRING TEAM

The Sharp Sales Director had not been at Fit Finance for very long. She knew it had been flagging for a while, so she decided a great place to start getting to the bottom of the problem would be to meet with Fit Finance's regional managers.

The Sharp Sales Director had already made one big and rather unsettling discovery. From her notes it was clear that, on an individual basis, each member of the regional team was more experienced than she. Indeed, each regional manager had a fearsome reputation as a brilliant and effective worker. They were the kings and queens of their respective domains.

How could Fit Finance be struggling with such big guns working for them? wondered the Sharp Sales Director.

When the Sharp Sales Director gathered them all round the boardroom table, she quickly discovered the problem. As she worked through the meeting agenda, all the managers expressed strong and differing views on every topic that came up – from which IT systems to prioritise, to how what hours should be worked each day, to how best to run promotions – they all had an opinion.

The regional managers bickered and argued and wasted time. They saw each other as rivals and took more pleasure in beating their colleagues than beating the competition.

Understanding that none of them would ever change, the Sharp Sales Director realised she would have to let a number go until they worked as a team.

People who cannot work
together cannot succeed together.

THE TRUSTING MANAGER
AND THE NEW TECHNOLOGY

The Trusting Manager at Logixtic knew how to get the best out of his team: he engaged them at every opportunity. If something needed to be done at the IT firm, he'd ask for their input, whether it was introducing a suggestion box to chairing a weekly discussion forum.

The team loved being included and they enjoyed the fact that the Trusting Manager gave them full authority to make decisions on their own account.

As a result, Logixtic became ever more productive and everyone benefitted.

Even so, the Trusting Manager was constantly wary about some new technology being developed elsewhere that might make their output redundant or cause a reduction in their workforce.

The Trusting Manager decided to share his worries and took some workers to see examples of the new technology in the country where it was being developed. The workers, on seeing the way the future was going, decided they would take control of managing the change. They ushered in the new developments, organised retraining and a voluntary redundancy programme.

Logixtic was the first business in the country to make use of the new technology and modernise and thus went from strength to strength. Competitors were far slower to adapt, with many managers springing the need for change on their workers and forcing things through. This lack of consultation created resentment and opposition and long-term issues.

Knowledge is power. When information is shared and responsibility entrusted, employees will shape their own future.

THE AUTOCRATIC MANAGER AND THE TASK

PhoneChamp, a large mobile phone business, recruited a new intake of managers. The group was to undertake a period of training and team-building before being sent out to their respective new posts. On the first day, the new managers were given a task to complete in groups.

In the first group, an Autocratic Manager immediately piped up and appointed herself team leader.

'I have done this before,' she declared. 'My friend is an expert in this area and my previous job required me to do it too. So it really is best if I take charge.'

Without waiting for a reply the Autocratic Manager set about telling everyone else what to do.

One or two of the more thoughtful members of the team spoke up to say perhaps it was a good idea to ask for some more information and perhaps pool ideas.

'There's no need, really, speed is of the essence and I know what to do,' the Autocratic Manager confidently asserted.

And the group carried on.

To the Autocratic Manager's surprise, her team's work

was assessed poorly against the other groups given a similar task. The bosses at PhoneChamp said they were very sorry to observe that the Autocratic Manager had given out over four hundred pieces of information and instructions and asked for none.

Elsewhere, the most successful team members had asked for around five pieces of information before giving a response and coming to a collective view.

A team will always perform better than an
individual when allowed and encouraged to do so!

THE RESOURCEFUL MANAGING DIRECTOR AND THE COMMON ENEMY

'We hate marketing,' confided a fed-up commercial executive. 'Why should they tell us what promotions to run?'

'We hate retail,' said a disgruntled marketer. 'We want to run promotions and they tell us they can't work to our timetable. Why do they always need more time?'

'We hate the supply chain,' fumed the testy retailer. 'They can never give us the right stock at the right time to run successful promotions.'

'We hate services,' griped the supply chain boss. 'We need more space to run extra promotions and they say they can't build it because they are too busy.'

'We hate personnel,' grumbled the discontented man from services. 'We need extra hours to complete the building requests, but they won't give us the go ahead.'

'We hate IT,' moaned the irritated personnel manager. 'We need systems support to allow us to build an overtime system so that services and others can do more.'

'We hate commercial,' hissed the cranky IT executive. 'They never seem to be able to get their act together on promotions and give us a clear brief.'

The Resourceful Managing Director listened carefully and resisted the temptation to put her head in her hands. She knew what she had to do to calm her warring department heads.

The Resourceful Managing Director revealed that she had heard that their largest rival was planning a big promotional push and that nobody knew what it was. She indicated that she was fearful what that could mean for jobs and bonuses and that everyone needed to get their own plans in place quickly or risk being out competed. Feeling threatened by the competitor, the departments stopped complaining about each other and worked together to counter the unknown threat.

To unify and focus a team, create a common
goal, or threat, to be met or countered.

CHAPTER EIGHT

The art of communication

THE SELF-IMPORTANT FOUNDER AND THE NEWSPAPER

After a decade at the top of Big Corp, the Self-Important Founder was rather pleased with himself. Everyone told him that his company was the biggest and the best, customers loved his goods and important people clamoured to meet him and ask how he had managed to do such a great job. He even boasted that he had the ear of the Prime Minister herself.

The Self-Important Founder was astonished when he picked up his daily newspaper and saw a banner headline declaring a problem at Big Corp. This had never happened before.

'How dare they write these terrible things about me and my company,' he stormed. 'Do they not know how many jobs I have created, how much tax we have paid and how much my customers love us! We are a brilliant and powerful company.'

'I will show them not to mess with me,' he said and immediately phoned the journalist responsible for the rude article and let rip.

'But it's a legitimate story, there was a problem,' explained the journalist calmly. 'Writing about these things is my job.'

'You'll pay for this. I know lots of very important people,' screamed the Self-Important Founder, slamming the phone down.

Word of the incident spread and journalists wondered what else the Self-Important Founder had to hide. Nothing else could explain his extreme reaction. Soon other unflattering stories began to appear and, in no time at all, Big Corp struggled to get any good press at all. Customers read their newspapers and began to wonder if Big Corp was as good as they always thought it was.

Hubris can be costly.

THE TALENTED JEWELLER AND THE SILLY JOKE

The Talented Jeweller worked for many, many years to build a large and successful jewellery business committed to competitive prices. He was as pleasant as he was clever and had a good sense of humour. The Talented Jeweller would often joke with his closest friends that the reason he could sell his wares at such low prices was because some of what he sold was rubbish. His friends knew he didn't really mean it. He was a modest man and was passionate about his business.

One day the Talented Jeweller had to make a speech to financial analysts and the press. Such events are often quite staid and boring and to lighten the mood he repeated his self-deprecating joke. After all, it had got many chuckles before and the talented owner was trying to be modest about his success.

The following day everybody was talking about the Talented Jeweller. The newspapers had run a story repeating the Talented Jeweller's words. They told their readers that the Talented Jeweller had said his shops sold cheap goods because they were rubbish!

Over night people stopped shopping at his stores because

they did not want to be seen as foolish or cheap. Before long, the business had to close and thousands of jobs were lost.

Think before you speak –
never joke about your livelihood.

THE TIRED MANAGER
AND THE AWARD

While winning an award is always flattering, the Tired Manager was not happy. In order to accept the prestigious gong for services to the construction industry, he would have to speak at a special awards dinner. It was not the engagement he minded, but simply that it was occurring at the end of a long week and he knew these things often dragged on far into the night. The Tired Manager would far rather go home to begin his weekend.

The bosses at Cemexa insisted the Tired Manager went. His colleagues at Cemexa insisted too. And so did the Cemexa PR folk.

So, the Tired Manager went to the ceremony.

The Tired Manager was in a poor mood when he arrived at the posh hotel for the dinner and eager for the evening to be over. The first thing he asked his host was how early he could leave and throughout dinner he kept checking his phone and huffing and puffing about not being at home with his family.

After his speech, the Tired Manager was given a generous vote of thanks and the award to recognise his achievements. But still he couldn't wait to leave. He pushed his way out of the dinner and moaned and quipped about how tacky the award was, how rubbish the food and how inane the questions.

Everyone who heard his reaction was shocked. It was all anyone could talk about for the rest of evening and in the following days it hit the press. Sentiment towards the Tired Manager and Cemexa turned sour.

'Don't go there,' people would say. 'They are far too self-important.'

The awards people certainly did not trouble the company again.

When on parade never let your true feelings show – no matter how tired or frustrated you feel!

THE SHORT-TEMPERED ENTREPRENEUR AND THE NEGATIVE STORY

An investigative journalist wrote a story in the newspaper about how terrible it was that Big Bux was importing products from a country that had a poor human rights record.

The Short-Tempered Entrepreneur was furious. He had plunged his life-savings into Big Bux and spent years working hard to make the company a success. Who was this journalist to make such ill-informed accusations?

The Short-Tempered Entrepreneur immediately picked up the phone to berate the journalist and explain that the business had been importing products from the same small village for decades.

'Without this contract the villagers would go hungry,' he fumed.

The journalist agreed this was the case, but questioned the Short-Tempered Entrepreneur about why he still traded in this country when so many companies chose not to.

The Short-Tempered Entrepreneur did not answer the question and instead spoke harshly to the journalist about how they were missing the point. Nothing was resolved and the journalist continued to write negative stories about Big Bux.

The Short-Tempered Entrepreneur became so angry he immediately stopped all of his advertising with the newspaper. His colleagues warned him that it was not a good idea, but he refused to listen.

The newspaper's owners were unrepentant. With no advertising revenue to protect, they allowed their journalists and editors to look for even more negative stories about Big Bux. It didn't take long before other newspapers were alerted to potential problems at Big Bux.

The Short-Tempered Entrepreneur could not understand what had gone so wrong. As profits plunged, the suppliers in the small village began to go hungry.

Listen to criticism and be reasonable –
if you are mortally offended, withdraw slowly,
politely and with grace.

THE TIDY MANAGER AND THE HIGH STANDARDS

The Tidy Manager always told anyone who would listen that he had the highest possible standards.

'Wherever I work, I see to it that everything is top notch,' he said.

The Managing Director of the House Beautiful department store had high hopes when he employed the Tidy Manager, especially after he heard his speech about standards. After a few weeks, he visited him in his busy department to see how he was getting along.

The sales floor looked a mess. Most worryingly, there was a tower of shopping baskets next to the till that was leaning so much to one side they seemed to be defying gravity. Worse still, the young man on the till was lobbing still more baskets to the top of the stack. The managing director called over the Tidy Manager.

'Didn't you tell me you have high standards?' said the Managing Director.

'Indeed,' nodded the Tidy Manager. 'The highest.'

The Managing Director looked confused and asked;

'So, tell me, what are your standards for baskets by the till?'

The Tidy Manager, who had his back to the till said: 'They need to be neat and tidy.'

'What does neat and tidy mean?' pressed the Managing Director.

'Well, I suppose all the handles should face the same way, there shouldn't be any litter or stock in the baskets and, when the stack reaches the height of the till, someone should take them to the entrance,' explained the Tidy Manager.

Turning the Tidy Manager around to see the leaning tower of baskets the Managing Director asked: 'Does your team know what you mean by "neat and tidy"?'

The Tidy Manager shook his head. Looking around he saw all the poor standards his team had failed to notice because he had never explained exactly what he meant.

If you are not clear and specific
about the standards required, how can
you expect your team to be?

THE KEEN YOUNG NEWCOMER AND THE LEASE

The Keen Young Newcomer felt nervous and excited to be presenting a paper to the Taxavo board on its lease extension. He'd not been at the large accountancy firm for long and he knew this was his moment to shine.

As the Keen Young Newcomer took a chair at the end of the table, the Chairman congratulated him on the paper and deal. Fully expecting the agreement to be nodded through, the Chairman asked if there were any questions.

There was just one.

'Do you think this the best length of time we could negotiate?' a board member asked.

The Keen Young Newcomer saw his chance to impress. Instead of saying 'yes', he launched into a long-winded explanation of absolutely everything he knew about property. He talked about discount rates, yields, covenants and ownership structures. Everything.

His lengthy speech prompted another board member to ask if it wasn't better to try and buy the freehold, rather than extend a lease.

And off the Keen Young Newcomer went, with another long and detailed explanation. Each time he did this, it prompted another question.

Eventually, after more than two hours analysing a deal that could have been agreed in moments, the Chairman drew the conversation to a close. He asked the Keen Young Newcomer to go away and come back with a revised paper taking into account all the issues raised at the meeting.

One month later, a revised paper came back. It was ten times as long as before, with every nuance of the deal and options set out. The board readily agreed the originally proposed plan.

Answer the question you
are asked. It always saves time.

THE BUSY JUNIOR MANAGERS AND THE IMPORTANT MEETING

At the Babel Inc informal pre-meeting, the Busy Junior Managers were to agree what should be agreed at the meeting and what sign off they would need from their bosses. They didn't want to waste time after all.

When the pre-meeting started, each of the Busy Junior Managers took time to agree the agenda and the exact order in which things would be discussed. They also took the opportunity to agree what time they should have breaks during the meeting.

Next the Busy Junior Managers agreed that they should have presented the pre-circulated pack for each agenda item to make sure they were all up to speed. And so for each agenda item the presenter turned the pages on the pack everyone should have already read.

As not everyone present had their bosses agreement to what needed to be agreed, it was decided to ask their bosses what should now be covered at the next meeting in order to move towards a decision. Furthermore not all the Busy Junior Managers present had the authority to be able to sign off on decisions in the light of new information raised at the meeting from their colleagues in other departments. All agreed and new dates were set for another informal pre-meeting and a meeting!

When all is said and done,
a lot more is said than done!

THE DISTRAUGHT CHIEF EXECUTIVE AND THE CHEMICAL SPILL

There was once a massive leak from a pipe on a huge industrial estate. Tons of toxic chemicals poured into a once beautiful river and all along the riverbank fish, birds and other wildlife lay dead or dying.

The story became huge news as other businesses along the river were affected, fishermen lost their livelihoods and the tourist trade was decimated.

The Distraught Chief Executive of the chemical company travelled to the scene and spent days and days briefing politicians, visiting the local villages and the spill site. The Distraught Chief Executive was put under enormous pressure from environmentalists and affected locals. He became the person to blame and at every turn microphones were put under his nose as people demanded an explanation about what had happened and what he was going to do about the mess, loss of jobs and livelihoods.

One day, exhausted and missing his family, the Distraught Chief Executive blurted out to a reporter: 'I just want to get back to normal. It's been a terrible experience for me. I haven't stopped.'

The locals went mad, as did the environmentalists and politicians.

'How dare he say that when our lives are ruined!' they all shouted.

Now the chemical company was really going to pay. People boycotted the company and politicians planned huge fines.

Always consider others before yourself.

THE BOASTFUL AD-MAN AND HIS CHICKENS

A group of leading businessmen sat around at dinner talking about all things business. One of the party, an expert in advertising, was very keen to let the others know how successful he was.

When he overheard a neighbour ask another guest how many chickens he had, the Boastful Ad-Man saw a chance to impress and jumped straight in.

'I have chickens,' he announced, oblivious to the quizzical stares at his interruption.

'Oh, how many chickens do you have?' responded his neighbour politely.

'Thirteen, actually, at my country home. They give me at least ten eggs a day. There is nothing like having your own eggs for breakfast. I am thinking of getting a few more hens in fact. They have quite a big enclosure now but I will probably need to enlarge it.'

The Boastful Ad-Man bored on and on about his chickens, what they ate and where they slept.

When he had blown himself out the Boastful Ad-Man finally thought to ask the other guest how many chickens he had.

'About fifteen million,' replied the man nonchalantly.

'He is the biggest egg producer in the UK,' added the neighbour.

The advertising man suddenly felt very small.

Beware of foolish boasting.
Know your audience first!

THE AFFABLE CHAIRMAN AND THE TRUSTING RIVALS

Everyone knew and liked the Affable Chairman. Whenever he ran into his competitors at industry events, he was always quick to compliment them on how well they were all doing. The Affable Chairman played down his own company's successes and instead asked how his rivals managed to achieve so much.

The rivals for their part were flattered. They didn't see the Affable Chairman as a threat, even though they operated in the same sector. As a result, they would talk openly about their plans, the competition and the market. The Affable Chairman gleaned lots of helpful information in this way.

When the Affable Chairman's competitors needed to sell off parts of their business, they all first turned to the man they trusted. They were even prepared to sell for less money than they'd expect from other firms. Rather than shout, or gloat about his good fortune, the Affable Chairman kept quiet. This, in turn, landed even more prizes in his lap.

People love to talk about themselves and
their achievements. Encourage them!

CHAPTER NINE

Marketing and making
an impression

THE PROMOTIONS ORGANISER
AND THE FREE FLIGHTS

The Promotions Organiser was always on the look out for a clever idea. She worked for an electronics firm called Vaxso and there never seemed to be anything truly exciting happening in her field.

One day, she was chatting to a friend who worked for an airline. She learnt that, on average, planes flew with 30 per cent of the seats empty.

'Even if we got £10 a ticket for those seats, it would be worth it,' said the airline woman.

The Promotions Organiser had an idea. She suggested to the bosses of Vaxso that if someone bought one of their products, they would be offered a free flight. She could do a deal with the airline to buy up the unsold capacity at a bargain price, but at least the airline would have some money and customers would get used to flying with them. It was win, win for everyone. The bosses loved the idea!

And, as she expected, customers loved the promotion. In fact, they loved it so much, they even bought one of Vaxso's products *just* so they'd get the free flight. After all, they could spend just a hundred pounds or so on something they didn't necessarily need and then fly anywhere in the world.

Soon, it got out of control. Vaxso's factory could not keep up with demand. The airline's booking system collapsed and it became almost impossible to book the free flights due to unprecedented demand. Regular passengers prepared to pay the full fare were furious, too because they were unable to book seats as they'd been snapped up by the promotion hunters.

Unravelling the clever idea cost millions in compensation to fed-up customers, many of whom never ever forgave Vaxso, or the airline.

> *Beware offering unlimited promotions when capacity is finite – you may do more damage than good to your reputation.*

THE QUICK-WITTED AD-MAN
AND THE TRAINS

The Quick-Witted Ad-Man was pitching to win the business of Shuttle, a newly privatised state-owned railway. He arranged for Shuttle's Chairman to visit the agency offices at midday for a pitch, which was to be followed by lunch at a nice restaurant.

Shuttle's chauffeur-driven Chairman arrived promptly at the Quick-Witted Ad-Man's offices but was rather unimpressed to be kept waiting by the receptionist who was chatting on the phone and ignoring him. When she had finished her conversation, the Shuttle Chairman introduced himself and explained why he was there. The receptionist waved him to the waiting area as she made another call.

The waiting area was a mess. Crumpled newspapers were spread over the seats and there were half-empty cups of coffee, chocolate wrappers and crisp packets on the table. There were even empty beer cans discarded on the floor.

The Chairman did his best to make himself comfortable while he waited. And waited. Ten minutes turned into fifteen, then twenty. After twenty-five minutes the Chairman stormed back to the reception desk to demand to know why he was being kept waiting. The receptionist shrugged her shoulders and offered to bring over a coffee.

Finally, after another long wait, the Chairman snapped and stood up to leave. As he did so the Quick-Witted Ad-Man walked in. He had been eyeing events through a keyhole all along.

'Now you have witnessed at first-hand what your customers endure, I think it's time I took you for a good lunch so we can talk about how we can put it right,' said the Quick-Witted Ad-Man.

Experiencing what others
experience focuses the mind.

THE ATTENTIVE OWNER WHO TRIED TO PLEASE EVERYONE

The Attentive Owner of the CarSmart car showroom was always eager to please. When customers demanded cheaper prices, he thought about it long and hard. How could he do it and still stay in business?

I know, thought the Attentive Owner. *We can reduce our prices if we sell a smaller range of cars, as long as we sell a lot more of the ones we still stock.*

So CarSmart cut its range and prices. But, to the Attentive Owner's surprise, customers started to go elsewhere, because the shop no longer sold their favourite products.

We will cut prices further, thought the Attentive Owner. *That will get them back*.

To achieve this, the Attentive Owner had to cut the number of staff that manned the CarSmart sales floor.

Sure enough, prices were cut as the pay bill shrunk, but even more customers started to disappear since they no longer received the service they were used to. CarSmart looked less well cared for and customers begrudged waiting to get help from a sales executive.

We'll cut the quality of what we sell, thought the Attentive Owner. *That way we can charge even less.*

And he did.

But customers then said, 'CarSmart has nothing good to offer us.'

They never shopped at CarSmart again.

Just cheap is never enough.

THE INNOCENT ENTREPRENEUR
AND HIS RESTAURANT

Running the Happy Eats Restaurant was an entirely new experience for the Innocent Entrepreneur. He'd never run a business before and only fell into running the eatery because he'd inherited it from a family member. Still, restaurant experience or no restaurant experience, the Innocent Entrepreneur was determined to make a go of things.

The Innocent Entrepreneur invested every penny he had in a new kitchen and an expensive redecoration of the Happy Eats Restaurant. To finish it off, he employed a top chef and a team of experienced waiting staff.

The Innocent Entrepreneur felt certain his restaurant would be a runaway success. But each night he waited for diners to come in. And each night he looked around at empty tables and empty chairs. Until one evening he had an idea.

If I make the restaurant seem full, then people will want to come in, he thought.

So the Innocent Entrepreneur invited his family and friends for breakfast, lunch and dinner.

'Eat as much as you like, it's all free,' he told them.

He treated them to the best champagne and wine too. Sure enough, other diners started to arrive and the Innocent Entrepreneur was happy that his restaurant was finally flourishing.

Yet, at the end of the first month, when the Innocent Entrepreneur counted his takings, he found he was losing money. A lot of money.

The bank agreed to lend the Innocent Entrepreneur money to tide him over.

However, the bank warned: 'Stop feeding your family and friends for free. If you don't, the bank will take the restaurant.'

But while the Innocent Entrepreneur had the best intentions, he couldn't stop himself from hosting his friends and family. Besides, each evening the restaurant was packed and full of music and laughter.

At the end of the year the Innocent Entrepreneur was unable to settle the overdraft and was forced to close the Happy Eats Restaurant. The bank took possession and the owner was left with nothing.

There is little room for unprofitable
generosity in any business.

THE THRIFTY BUYER
AND THE CARRIER BAGS

The Thrifty Buyer wanted to impress her bosses at the big supermarket chain GrocerLargo. Luckily, she had a great idea. GrocerLargo used to give away millions of carrier bags a year, but now customers were required by law to pay for them. What if she, the Thrifty Buyer, could get the carrier bags dirt cheap? Then the supermarket would make a tidy profit on each bag.

The Thrifty Buyer scoured the world and found a supplier who could sell her a bulk order of carrier bags at almost half the cost of their current suppler. Perfect!

The Thrifty Buyer agreed the order and the carrier bags arrived on time, in large containers. There was enough for a whole year.

But, very soon after they were sent out to the GrocerLargo shops, customers complained that the bags ripped and the handles broke when filled to the brim. While the bags looked similar, they were not as well made. Soon GrocerLargo customers had to use almost twice as many half-loaded carrier bags and they were very cross because they had to pay for each one. GrocerLargo was inundated with complaints about something most customers had barely noticed just a short while before.

Sometimes the lowest cost isn't the best.

THE DIPLOMATIC EXECUTIVE
AND THE FACE MASK

The Diplomatic Executive was very anxious about his meeting in Tokyo. He was to spend the morning with the president of the company that his business supplied and he was eager not to cause offence. The Diplomatic Executive listened intently as his guide and interpreter give him a briefing on all the required etiquette, such as when and how to bow, the accepted way to exchange business cards and so on. It all felt like a bit of a minefield, but by the time he entered the meeting room, the Diplomatic Executive was confident he had the basics right.

The Diplomatic Executive was somewhat taken aback, however, when the Japanese President entered the room wearing a surgical face mask and white cotton gloves. The westerner did his best not to show his annoyance at this apparent insult as they bowed, exchanged cards and began their discussions. The President never once removed his face mask as the conversation was translated back and forth.

The meeting ended promptly with another bow and a handshake.

Once outside the building the Diplomatic Executive told

the guide he was unimpressed that the President had worn a mask and gloves.

'Does he think I am carrying some dreadful germs?' he fumed

'Oh no,' said the guide, who was genuinely alarmed. 'The President had a cold and was wearing the mask and gloves out of respect for you, so *you* didn't catch any germs.'

Do not judge others by your own customs.

THE CONFUSED COUPLE AND A REASON TO BUY

The Confused Couple couldn't decide whether to buy the product they wanted from one shop or the other. The products looked so similar and the prices were identical. The Confused Couple told the first shopkeeper that they couldn't make up their minds whether to buy from him, or his competitor. To try and win the business, the shopkeeper offered them a 10 per cent discount.

The Confused Couple thanked him, but said they needed time to think. They left to go and see what the competitor could do.

Once at the competitor's shop, the Confused Couple explained the discount they had been offered. The cunning shopkeeper smiled, for he knew exactly what to do.

'I'm afraid I can't give you a discount as the product in my shop is the newest design with some improvements,' he said smoothly.

He then gave a broad smile and added: 'But there is a promotion whereby each one comes with a free pen.'

The Confused Couple didn't hesitate to complete the

purchase. The newest design with some improvements! And they had got a free pen with it, too. They went away smiling.

There are more ways to sell
than dropping the price.

THE DESPONDENT MARKETEER AND THE OLD TOOTHPASTE

The Despondent Marketeer sat slumped at her desk looking glum and holding a tube of toothpaste.

'What's up with you?' asked her more experienced neighbour.

'They have asked me to increase the sales of this old toothpaste,' explained the Despondent Marketeer. 'I haven't got a clue where to start. It was first launched ten years ago and sales have been falling ever since.'

'Easy,' said a colleague, 'you need to run a big promotion. Halve the price to get people buying the toothpaste again.'

So that is exactly what she did and sales did increase through the promotion. Not enough, though, to cover the cost of selling the toothpaste for half price though.

'You need a different plan,' advised another colleague. 'Think of a simple improvement. Then give some away for free. Trust me.'

The Despondent Marketeer did as advised and took the old toothpaste to the laboratory.

He got them to add some fresh mint to the formula and

then went to see the technical department and asked if the tube could be made larger. It could.

The Despondent Marketeer relaunched the toothpaste as 'new and improved' with '33% extra free'. Sales rocketed, far exceeding budget.

> *New and free are the two most powerful*
> *words in consumer marketing*

CHAPTER TEN

Lead, follow, or get out of the way

THE RECKLESS MANAGER AND THE ONCE POSH HOTEL

The Reckless Manager was very clear in his instructions to his marketing manager.

'It's make or break time for the Dreams hotel,' he declared. 'Our rooms need to hit 70 per cent occupancy.'

The Marketing Manager ran a promotion advertising that Dreams' prices would be reduced by a third. The posh hotel was nearly fully booked as a result. The Reckless Manager was very pleased, but confused when he saw profits were down rather than up over the same period last year.

Digging around, the Reckless Manager discovered that some of his best customers, who normally paid full price, had taken advantage of the general discount, or couldn't get a room as the hotel was so busy and so he'd lost money there. Takings per person in the Dreams bar and restaurant had been less as the new customers were more frugal. So he'd made less money there. With a full hotel the staff bill was even higher than it was before. So he'd lost there too.

Worse still, following the promotion some of his regular customers who couldn't get a room had gone to a rival luxury hotel and had not returned. Others turned their noses up at the new residents staying at discounted prices and said the hotel was 'going downhill.'

The Reckless Manager decided to take another roll of the dice to achieve the coveted average of 70 per cent occupancy. He instructed the Marketing Manager to run another discount promotion to drive occupancy once more – which it did – but also asked the Purchasing Manger to cut the cost of the things Dreams used. The Purchasing Manager bought cheaper meat for the restaurant and snacks for the bar. The bed linen was downgraded, as well as the toiletries in the bathroom.

The regular guests soon noticed the lower quality and complained the loo roll was thinner, the soap smaller, the shampoo inferior and the bed linen less crisp.

After the promotion finished occupancy dropped below 50 per cent and profits plummeted. Staff numbers were cut and service standards fell, leading to even more of its regular customers going elsewhere. The once grand Dreams hotel eventually closed.

Attracting a different customer group with different expectations can do long-term harm.

THE UNDER-CONFIDENT MANAGER AND THE CAR OF THE YEAR

Everybody was speculating about who would win the much sought-after promotion at the utility giant Utium. Privately, many senior managers thought they would be a shoo-in for the job.

I'm great at logistics, so they are bound to choose me, thought one manager.

My marketing knowledge is unparalleled, thought another.

There is no one who can handle finance as well as me, contemplated another.

The Under-Confident Manager was one of the only senior executives who thought he didn't stand a chance.

I haven't shone at anything, he mused.

When the Utium board announced who had got the post, everyone was astonished. Unbelievable to all, it transpired that the Under-Confident Manager was being made their boss.

No one was more surprised than the Under-Confident Manager himself. He went to see the Utium board to find out why he had been promoted.

'But so-and-so is better than me at finance, and so-and-so is better at administration,' he explained, working through each of the potential candidates one by one and pointing out why they would be so much better for the job.

The Utium Chief Executive smiled and explained: 'The "Car of the Year" is rarely best on any specific dimension; whether it is fuel efficiency, design, handling or comfort. However, it is invariably in the top five of each of those categories. It is because of that consistency that it becomes "Car of the Year". It is your consistency and energy across all areas that single you out for promotion.'

To lead well, it is better to be consistently
good at many things, and acknowledge the specialist
skills of others, rather than be the best at just one.

THE ELDERLY INDUSTRIALIST
AND THE IMPORTANT INHERITANCE

The Elderly Industrialist was very keen that one of his four children took over the family factory, HollyNuts, when he retired.

As tradition dictates, he offered the role to his eldest son first, even though the young man had never shown any real interest in the business. With no practical experience of how it worked, or its people and processes, the eldest son found it difficult to make decisions and failed to win the respect of the other managers.

The eldest son was quite grateful when the second-born agreed to step-up to the plate.

She knew how things worked and had built close relationships with the team. They had seen her in the factory since she was a little girl, often fussing over her and calling her by a special nickname. Sadly, the second-born was too close to her staff and lacked the courage to direct the workforce to do what was required. She didn't want to hurt anyone's feelings.

The challenge fell to the next child. He'd seen his brother and sister fail and thought he knew what to do. So he ignored the advice of his managers and rubbed everyone up the wrong way through his arrogance. Before long, he too was asked to step down.

Finally, the Elderly Industrialist turned to his youngest child and gave her the responsibility. She had been following things very closely and had seen where her siblings had failed to deliver. Even though she hadn't spent time on the factory floor before, she made sure from that day on she made regular visits to learn the ins and outs of the business and to get to know the staff. However, she made sure to be independent enough so she could be free to make clear decisions. And finally, she remembered not to let it all go to her head.

Which was just as well, as the company went from strength to strength.

None of us are born leaders. Everyone takes
time to learn the fine balance of many qualities
that make a good leader.

THE ANXIOUS EXECUTIVE
WHO TRIED TO STAY ON TOP

As far as the Anxious Executive at Shining Light was concerned, his role was to be the golden star at the centre of the team and the other members were there to make him look good. Thus, the Anxious Executive always made sure that when he appointed people to his team, they were good but not too good; he should be the brightest.

After all, the leader should always be the best, he thought.

The Anxious Executive also made sure never to praise his team too highly in public. He didn't want other people to overhear such a thing and to think others were better than he.

Even when the Anxious Executive finally retired, he tried to take steps to ensure his successor was less good, so his own legacy looked greater.

But the New Executive was different.

Firstly, she recruited people who were far more knowledgeable than she was to head each department. She then publicly acknowledged how good each new team member was, actively seeking their advice and listening to their views.

The New Executive saw her role as creating the conditions

for the team to work together. The team enjoyed great success and the Anxious Executive's 'legacy' was quickly forgotten.

Confident leaders surround
themselves with very able people.

THE SECONDED TRAINEE
AND THE COACHING MANAGER

There was once an engineering firm, Sturtech, which ran an active training scheme for young managers. Each trainee was sent out to work for four weeks in every part of the company and the CEO took a genuine interest in their feedback on their return.

On the day the Seconded Trainee returned to the Sturtech head office, the CEO called him into his office.

'So, what did you learn from our factory in the north?' he asked the young man.

The Seconded Trainee looked thoughtful. 'Not a great deal,' he admitted. 'Don't get me wrong, the manager there was brilliant and had everything running like clockwork. He was in the business every day and always went through what to do in great detail while constantly checking up on the team. The thing is, if he was away for a day, no one knew what to do.'

It was the CEO's turn to look thoughtful.

'And what about our factory in the south?' he asked the Seconded Trainee.

'That was completely different,' the Seconded Trainee explained. 'The manager spent a lot of time with each member of staff explaining how to do things, why they were important and how to react to different events. He trusted them to get on with things. Even when he was away, things went perfectly smoothly.'

Teach don't tell.

THE MODEST CHAIRMAN'S THREE DECISIONS

The Young Executive felt flattered when he was seated next to the Chairman of one of the world's largest oil companies at an industry dinner.

'I just can't imagine how busy you must be and how many decisions you must make at Petrano,' said the Young Executive in awe.

'Not really,' replied the Modest Chairman. 'We have a great team of executives at Petrano who make all the main decisions about the running of the company. There are just three issues I have in my mind for this year.'

The Young Executive leaned in, waiting to hear what the Modest Chairman had to say.

The Modest Chairman explained that he needed to decide whether or not to withdraw operations from a troubled African country. He also had to figure out whether or not to invest in the technology to exploit shale gas, which meant being confident that the price of a barrel of oil would hit a certain price in ten years time. And lastly, he had to determine who might be the next CEO.

The Young Executive was surprised but recognised these three decisions were crucial to the future of the company. They were decisions only the Modest Chairman could make because of the long and short-term implications for shareholders.

Concentrate on what only you *can do.*

 # THE APATHETIC EXECUTIVE
WHO WAS ASLEEP ON THE JOB

If you saw him, you'd say the Apathetic Executive was doing just fine. He came to work on time at Just Enough and his department worked efficiently. Look closely, though, and you'd see he always left promptly at the end of the day and, while his department was doing OK, it never sparkled.

The Managing Director noticed, though, and arranged a meeting with the Apathetic Executive.

'Can you tell me what you do every day?' asked the Managing Director.

If the Apathetic Executive was surprised, he didn't show it.

'I get through around one hundred emails a day, which I always answer promptly, deal with the paper post and then, of course, there are phone calls and meetings,' he explained.

'Yes, that's fine, but what do you *do*?' pressed the Managing Director.

The Apathetic Executive looked nonplussed and repeated his list of chores again.

'But doing those things is the bare minimum in your role,' the Managing Director said impatiently. 'What makes a difference is what you do to make our business better each day. Being curious, agitating for things to be better and showing initiative. I am afraid you show none of those attributes so we will have to let you go.'

Completing administration efficiently
is just the start of an executive's role.

THE NEW LEADER AND THE DIFFICULT TEAM MEMBER

When the New Leader took over at Generations, an established family business, a few people on the team were curious. No one outside the founding family had ever led the firm before. Everyone felt a little unsettled by change, but one person in particular was furious as well. The Difficult Team Member had hoped for the job themselves.

I must make sure I unite the team, thought the New Leader.

When they all got together for the first time, the Difficult Team Member made some snide comments. However, the New Leader let them pass, thinking that it was better not to upset the apple cart.

Before long, the Difficult Team Member started to spend more time out of the office with his colleagues and used the opportunity to question the New Leader's judgement every chance he got.

When visiting more junior managers, the Difficult Team Member would roll his eyes and tut if the New Leader's ideas were discussed. He would invariably put forward a counter view. But in spite of feedback the New Leader did nothing.

The team and the entire Generations business was soon fractured and under-performing. The New Leader was asked to leave.

No business can serve two leaders.

THE FORWARD-THINKING MANAGING DIRECTOR AND THE BIG NEW PLAN

The Forward-Thinking Managing Director spent a long time with her board developing a Big New Plan to move the ailing company forward. The Big New Plan was ambitious and would take time, but she was confident it was a winner for the manufacturing giant, Mectech.

The Forward-Thinking Managing Director presented the Big New Plan to her colleagues and told them to get on with making it happen.

A short while later the Exasperated Factory Manager was knocking on the Forward-Thinking Managing Director's door to complain that many people didn't really understand the plan. People were also asking: 'How long will it take?'

The Forward-Thinking Managing Director explained it again and urged everyone to be patient.

Within a few months the Exasperated Factory Manager was back.

'Everyone keeps saying there are no noticeable changes,' she said. 'What shall I tell them?'

The Forward-Thinking Managing Director urged her to

tell everyone to be patient.

Before long, the Exasperated Factory Manager was back again. 'Everyone is very excited that the new equipment is finally getting a trial, but there seems to be an awful lot of teething problems,' she said.

The Forward-Thinking Managing Director urged her to tell everyone to be patient. She and her board were focused on getting things right, she explained.

The Exasperated Factory Manager returned again. 'I think most people have forgotten the new plan,' she said. 'They seem to be fixated on grumbling more than ever about their old and inefficient systems.'

By the time the new equipment was ready to be rolled out the Forward-Thinking Managing Director was under fire for the appalling state of the company's existing equipment. Everyone had forgotten her original Big New Plan. They were only concerned with how difficult their lives had been all this time.

Key messages need to be repeated and repeated to keep ideas fresh and alive. People see the point but forget.

THE ARTISTIC AND
SCIENTIFIC MANAGERS

There were once two managers who ran departments next to each other in the Automaestro car showroom. They were always keen to get the better of each other, which made for interesting times, since they had very different approaches to their jobs.

The Scientific Manager liked facts, numbers and research.

The Artistic Manager would look, listen, read and deduce before coming to a decision based on his experience and intuition.

One day their boss asked them to find out what their staff thought about extending trading hours each day.

The Scientific Manager issued a survey to her staff, asking them to score on a sliding scale how they felt about extending trading hours. The average was three out of five and so she declared the team broadly positive.

The Artistic Manager, by contrast, sat down with each member of staff and asked what they felt. Some younger members of staff said they would like the extra money but a number of experienced staff said it would be a real problem as they either had to pick up children or had complicated commutes.

The Artistic Manager concluded that the change would

potentially see some experienced staff leave and so the boss held off, thanking the Artistic Manager for his insightful information.

The boss then asked about whether the business served more male or female customers.

The Scientific Manager set up a questionnaire for the staff and at each transaction they recorded the sex of the customer, their age and when they shopped. The Scientific Manager found that 62 per cent of the customers were male, half were over thirty and that 12.23 pm was the busiest time for the business.

The Artistic Manager watched and listened and, at the end of the week, said he thought about two thirds of his customers were male and they visited mainly around lunchtime as they liked to browse and chat to other car enthusiasts.

The boss thanked them both but said the information about customers visiting to talk to other enthusiasts had been very helpful. The Artistic Manager felt quite pleased.

The boss then said she had a train to catch and asked the time. The Artistic Manager never wore a watch but deduced that it was probably after two and she knew there was a train around 4 o'clock-ish.

The Scientific Manager jumped in: 'It's 2.42 pm and you should be able to make the 3 o'clock train.'

The boss thanked her profusely. Then she turned to both managers as she was leaving. 'You have both done well but could be so much better if you could learn from each other. You need both accurate numbers and an understanding of what lies behind them to give your best.'

Both the art and the science of
business are required for success.

THE CONSISTENT PLAYER

The manager pondered who to promote at Lily Ponds. The first candidate had flashes of brilliance in design and sales whilst the second was consistently good and permanently determined at all things.

The manager chose the second, much to the other candidate's annoyance. He went to see his boss to ask why he had decided against him.

The manager knew the candidate to be a keen golfer and so explained: 'A good amateur golfer is able in a round to hit some shots as well as a professional. He may even drive the ball further on some occasions. But what marks out the professional is his ability to play consistently well shot after shot, round after round, week after week. So it is in business, keeping up your energy to consistently make good decisions and drive a team is what is required for long term success.'

The manager knew his boss was right and added determination and energy to his game and went on to enjoy great success.

Consistency in business is key.

CHAPTER ELEVEN

Culture is everything

THE GREEDY CEO, THE CAUTIOUS CEO AND THE SHARED TAKEOVER

The Greedy CEO of fashion chain Clothesy eyed the rival Glambelle chain covetously. He would give anything to get his hands on such a great brand. The trouble was, there was no way he could afford it.

The Greedy CEO thought and thought and eventually came up with a plan. What if he went into business with another fashion chain? They could offer to buy Glambelle half and half and share the spoils.

Excited by his idea, he went to speak to the Cautious CEO who ran the Ragbuy chain.

'That's an interesting idea,' agreed the Cautious CEO. 'I'm a bit worried though. If Ragbuy were to suddenly take on three hundred or so more shops, it would dramatically change the culture of the business. Besides, I don't have enough managers to run them the way I'd like.'

The Greedy CEO thought the Cautious CEO was very foolish but, seizing his chance, offered him an alternative plan.

'What if you just take a few stores? I'll do the whole deal and if you buy some of them, it'll help me fund it. Then you can buy more shops from me as and when you are ready with all your trained managers.'

So that is what they did. Over the next four years the Cautious CEO gradually bought around forty Glambelle shops from the Greedy CEO and each one was successfully integrated into his Ragbuy business.

Meanwhile the Greedy CEO's merger proved extremely difficult. It took a lot longer than he'd expected to convert the Glambelle shops into Clothsey ones and, meanwhile, the core business struggled as store managers and the central team were dragged into managing the merger. The deal almost brought Clothsey to its knees. The Greedy CEO left under a cloud.

Your company culture spreads with
its people, not with its assets.

THE WORLDLY WISE MANAGER AND THE LONG TRADITION

The Worldly Wise Manager felt sure he'd heard it all before. It seemed every company he'd worked at there were grand talks about culture and values. Yet these values could apparently be rewritten at a moment's notice when a new boss arrived and no one ever quite knew what a business stood for.

How different he found things at his new employers, the Sharing Partners, a company with a successful 150-year history behind it. On arrival the Worldly Wise Manager was trained on the history of the company, its values and the expectations of the staff. The same values had held good for decades and had been consistently applied. Instead of being given his management position straightway the Worldly Wise Manager first spent time as a trainee manager, on full manager's pay, shadowing an experienced manager so that he grew to understand how the theory of the Sharing Partners worked in practice.

Once it was felt the Worldly Wise Manager had absorbed enough, he was given his first shop to manage. At his first conference, to his complete amazement, the managing director asked the Worldly Wise Manager and the other first time attendees to stand. They were congratulated on their promotion and told of the responsibility they now held for their staff's well-being and happiness, the satisfaction of their customers and the maintenance of good relationships with their suppliers and the communities in which they traded. They were presented with a copy of the Sharing Partners' constitution, first written many decades before, which they were committed to uphold. Everyone felt the specialness of their position; every manager walked a foot taller.

Don't dismiss tradition – reminding people why what they do is special creates a powerful sense of purpose and pride.

THE NEW RECRUIT AND THE POWER OF LANGUAGE

The New Recruit had just finished her first morning at the smart department store.

'This is a lovely canteen,' said the New Recruit to her Department Manager as they queued for lunch.

The Department Manager nodded, smiled and asked: 'How was your first morning?'

'Good, although I only sold some cheap bits and pieces,' she replied. 'Oh, and I directed a number of customers to the toilets.'

The Department Manager smiled a knowing smile and they finished lunch.

'Is it OK if I have a quick look around the store before I go back to the department?' asked the New Recruit.

The Department Manager agreed and went back to work.

When the New Recruit returned, the Department Manager took her to one side.

'I think you have made an excellent start,' she began. 'But there is one thing I would like to talk to you about. We use slightly different language here. We have a staff dining room, not a canteen. We don't sell cheap things, rather they are inexpensive. We call toilets either the Ladies, or Gents, or washroom. And lastly, we work in a shop, not a store. You store things in stores, you sell things in shops.'

The internal language a business uses is important in setting tone and expectations.

THE AFFABLE OWNER AND THE CHECKER'S CHECKER'S CHECKER!

When the Affable Owner started One Step his motto was to keep things simple. He spent a lot of time dealing directly with his customers. It was his favourite part of the job. Sadly, as the business grew, he had less and less spare time to spend with his customers. In fact, it soon got to the stage where he had to recruit someone to take over his role in buying. Still, he trusted them to follow his lead and always do the right thing and took time to share all he knew. He wrote it down so all newcomers would understand.

The business continued to grow so the buyer had to recruit an assistant buyer. The Affable Owner met the assistant buyer and buyer routinely to make sure that the company principles were properly understood and maintained.

Soon the business was doing so well that the Affable Owner appointed a head buyer, promoting the buyer and assistant buyer and recruiting a replacement for the assistant. The owner now asked for a monthly report of what was happening as the business was so large he couldn't have meetings with everyone. He was, however, hopeful his values would continue.

But the business continued to get larger. With more growth,

the Affable Owner decided to break the business into three divisions. He still asked for monthly reports, which were now circulated to the Group Board, but trusted the structure and people he had put in place to make ethical decisions.

Eventually, it was time for the Affable Owner to retire and his business was lauded for its ethical approach. To ensure the culture the Affable Owner had so carefully nurtured stayed in place, his successor formed a new Ethics Committee to report to the Group Board. A detailed level of reporting signalled whether the company's history, procedures and culture were being maintained. The three divisions were then asked to set up steering groups and committees to provide reassurance to the Group Ethics Committee.

And so the Group Ethics Committee, supported by the Group Ethics Steering group, checked on the Divisions Ethics Committee, supported by the Divisional Ethics Steering Group, which checked on the Buying Ethics Group, which checked on the experienced head buyer, buyers and assistant buyers. Simplicity, just doing the right thing and trust became long-forgotten values.

Beware of bureaucracy for bureaucracy's sake.

THE TALENTED FOOTBALL MANAGER AND THE KIDS

When the Talented Football Manager arrived, the Ruff FC team was hanging on by its bootlaces to the last rung of the football league. The team was populated by old pros who struggled weekly to keep the team up for yet another season. They weren't very interested in the Talented Football Manager's ideas. They had heard it all before.

The Talented Football Manager could see there was no future in simply replacing the old pros each year and so he devoted his time and energy to the young teenagers in the Ruff FC junior team. He took over their training sessions, attended their matches and asked his scouts to search for the best young kids, rather than professionals near the end of their careers. The Talented Football Manager invested almost all his time in his fledglings, caring for every aspect of their footballing and personal development. He promised that if they made the grade, they would be playing in the Ruff FC first team from an early age, whereas if they went to a big club they would likely be in the reserves for many years. He also said he would gladly release them to a bigger club when they were approached.

The Talented Football Manager's plan worked! He began to feed the youngsters into the team. They were well tutored, worked as a team and were skilful. Ruff FC started to climb the league and the young players were spotted by bigger clubs. Good to his word, the Talented Football Manager willingly sold them on. As a result, the most talented young kids wanted to sign for Ruff FC and their parents were happy for them to do so. The quality of the team just kept improving and so the rise to the top continued.

To change a failing culture,
invest in the future generation.

THE CHARISMATIC CHAIRMAN AND THE FAVOURITES

There was once a company where everyone felt unhappy. At ClosedCo everyone vied for their Charismatic Chairman's attention, but few seemed to get it.

People would gossip in corners claiming to know the names of the Charismatic Chairman's favourites. They knew 'for sure' that he liked three people out of his team of eight the best. He would confide in them about the others, share his plans and talk to them daily.

Whether it was true or not, the other 'unfavoured' team members felt left out. Frustration in the team built and built, different camps formed and divisions grew and grew. When the Charismatic Chairman left, those close to him felt let down, while those excluded hoped their new chairman would listen to them and value their opinions and contribution.

And so it was. The Brand New Boss definitely had no favourites, valued everyone's views and never ever talked negatively to the other team members about their colleagues. Instead he praised each individual's successes. As a result the team grew to be united and harmonious and with a newfound confidence trusted each other, which led to open and honest discussions. The business enjoyed great results as a consequence.

Have no favourites and
treat all people equally.

THE INSIGHTFUL BOSS AND HIS BIG TOUR

The Area Manager was a little surprised when the newly appointed Insightful Boss asked him to arrange a tour of the best Trolley Dash store in his group. It was the first thing he wanted to do. The Area Manager felt confident that the selected Trolley Dash shop manager would make sure the shop was fully prepared, looked spick and span and was ready for the Big Tour. So confident was the Area Manager, he told the Insightful Boss it had been almost impossible to decide on which shop to pick in his group as all were of such a high standard!

The Insightful Boss smiled, he knew his plan would work!

On arriving in the car park, the Insightful Boss called the Area Manager to meet him there. He then meticulously checked the details of the whole operation, from the car park flower beds, to the Trolley Dash entrance, to the shop floor, warehouse and offices. The Insightful Boss praised things that were good and pointed out areas where things could be even better. And the Area Manager was forced to agree.

Once he had completed his Big Tour, the Insightful Manager thanked everyone and said he was extremely pleased with the standards they had set. He told the Area Manager he was delighted with the standards he had seen and even happier to learn that these would be replicated in all branches. He said that he would feedback on his future visits where the standards fell short.

The Area Manager now had a clear benchmark and had set himself the highest standards for all his shops.

Start by improving the best.
It raises the bar for all.

THE INEXPERIENCED SALESMAN ABROAD

The Inexperienced Salesman had not been with Admeria, a large advertising firm, for long, when he was very excited to secure a meeting with the senior management of a Japanese company that he knew his new bosses were very keen to work with.

He went straight to the prospective client's offices, well before the appointed time and was met at reception by a young woman who introduced herself and explained she had joined the company as a graduate the year previously. She now held a junior management position in the marketing department. She spoke good English and, on the way to the meeting room, the Inexperienced Salesman asked her lots about what she and her colleagues did in order to get some market background.

On entering the large boardroom, the Inexperienced Salesman bowed and exchanged business cards with six executives and then sat opposite them at the table with his interpreter. The young Japanese woman stood behind the six executives.

The conversation bounced to and fro through the interpreter. Then the Inexperienced Salesman turned directly to the young woman and asked her a direct question. The room fell deadly quiet. The Japanese executives exchanged surprised glances.

The Inexperienced Salesman repeated the question. The young woman looked horrified and remained silent. The interpreter broke in to advise the Inexperienced Salesman to ask one of the executives another question, which he did. The meeting bumbled on for a little while longer before being brought to an abrupt close.

Outside, the interpreter ticked off the Inexperienced Salesman for embarrassing the senior executives and the young woman. It was not the done thing to ask such a junior person a question at a meeting with the company's senior management. It was a cultural mistake. Not surprisingly, no order was secured from the company.

Understand and adapt to the culture
of those you are working with.

THE MICRO MANAGER AND THE WRONG LIST

The Micro Manager was famed throughout the bank for his attention to detail and he was very proud of the accolade. He would sign off each Banquo cheque and invoice personally and sign every pay sheet and holiday request.

The Micro Manager's desk was always piled with papers to review. He spent long hours making sure every bit of paper had his personal attention.

One day Banquo's Managing Director came down to the Micro Manager's office and took him for a walk.

'You are very diligent with your paperwork,' the Managing Director said as they walked.

'Thank you, I work through my list of what's to be done every day because I think it important to pay attention to detail,' responded the Micro Manager proudly.

'Hmmmm,' murmured the Managing Director. 'But, is it the right detail?'

And then, as they walked, the Managing Director pointed out that Banquo was failing to achieve its potential because there was much detail the Micro Manager failed to notice: the customers left queuing, the untidy counters, the mood and conditions of his staff.

Focus on the detail that
makes a commercial difference

CHAPTER TWELVE

Decision-making – good, bad and indifferent

THE PONDERING ENTREPRENEUR AND THE LONG DECISION

There were once four friends who decided to go into business together. They were very excited and had been talking about it for years and years and now they were finally taking the plunge and starting their very own artisan food business: Nutrelo.

Each of the friends had a job to do. One of them had to find a good property for the Nutrelo factory. Another had to sort out all the marketing, packaging and promotions and another was in charge of selling Nutrelo's food range.

That left the finances, which were down to the Pondering Entrepreneur. The Pondering Entrepreneur was a naturally cautious man and wanted to get everything 100 per cent right. Now they were spending their own money, there was no room for error.

'I just can't decide whether I agree with this budget or not,' said the Pondering Entrepreneur. 'I will need time to think it over.'

The days and weeks passed and the Pondering Entrepreneur kept on thinking.

'But we will lose a really good site if we don't act now,' said the Property Entrepreneur.

'And I need to place orders now for summer merchandise,' added the Marketing Entrepreneur.

'And I must commit now to our new clients,' said the Sales Entrepreneur.

But the Pondering Entrepreneur kept thinking. Eventually, after much pushing, the budget was agreed, but by then the great site was lost, the summer merchandise late and the client had gone elsewhere.

Promptitude is extremely desirable.

THE FRUGAL FINANCE DIRECTOR AND THE NEW FACTORY

No expense was spared when a new factory was built for Stax. The building was the biggest money could buy, with the best fittings and the best facilities. Everyone was very excited to be working there.

That is, except for the Frugal Finance Director.

'We've overspent our budget,' he complained.

Nobody at Stax really listened. After all, it was the Frugal Finance Director's job to moan about money, wasn't it?

Six months after the new factory opened, the bosses at Stax were alarmed to see that production was well below expectations. In fact, it was lower than when they worked in their previous antiquated and small factory.

They looked into the problem and discovered that the new factory manager who had been employed to run the unit was hopelessly out of his depth.

'Why on earth did we employ this man?' they demanded to know.

'Because the Frugal Finance Director said there was no budget left,' the unhappy human resources person replied.

'He was the best we could get for the money.'

> *Making a huge investment in assets*
> *and then skimping on the best managers*
> *is a foolish saving.*

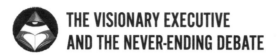

THE VISIONARY EXECUTIVE
AND THE NEVER-ENDING DEBATE

The Visionary Executive approached the GroCer board with the idea that its shops should be offering car washing as a service in their car parks.

'I'm not sure I want to manage that – trade could be very inconsistent,' said the Retail Director doubtfully.

'We don't have a ready water supply,' added the Services Director, 'or a shelter.'

'I'm not sure I could recruit the right people to work the right hours,' cut in the HR Director.

'And what costs will we incur and how many cars will we wash a week, at what price?' queried the Finance Director.

'I wonder if it might inconvenience customers who want a space simply to go shopping,' opined the Marketing Director.

Only the Commercial Director could see value in the Visionary Executive's proposal. However he wanted to be sure the service standard matched that of the GroCer shops.

'Why don't we outsource?' he suggested.

'Because then we will lose control of quality and service,' argued the Retail Director.

'And we potentially won't make as much money taking a commission on sales rather than the full profit if we did it ourselves,' said the Finance Director.

The Visionary Executive listened to all the comments and then asked the team to go away and think about how they might resolve the issues raised.

Meeting after meeting the debate raged, with board members variously arguing that customers either would, or wouldn't, like the service, whether a profit could, or couldn't, be made and whether the service should be run internally or externally. The conversation went on and on until everyone was so bored with the idea that they decided to put it to one side.

Until you try you'll never know.
Test instead of debating.

THE WORRIED SHOPKEEPER
AND THE ENDURING PROBLEM

Vintage, an antique shop in the centre of town was always a popular destination. It sold all sorts of interesting goods and its regular customers liked to pop in and see the new stock. They liked to have a chat with the owner too, because he was very knowledgeable about his trade. However, he often seemed a little distracted.

This is because he was a big worrier.

'I don't know what to do,' said the Worried Shopkeeper to himself when he came across one problem that he found particularly vexing. He had a big decision to make but couldn't decide which way he should go.

In his mind, the problem got bigger and bigger every day. Desperate for an answer, the Worried Shopkeeper shared the issue with more and more people. His colleagues at Vintage, as well as family and friends, all heard about the problem. Weeks went by but still the Worried Shopkeeper agonised about the decision.

Eventually, a good friend who also happened to be a successful businessman went to see the Worried Shopkeeper with a suggestion.

'You've been worrying about this problem for weeks,' the businessman said.

'That's because I want to make the right decision,' the Worried Shopkeeper responded.

'But any decision is better than no decision,' responded the businessman. 'You can learn from a wrong decision and benefit from a good one.'

> *Do something, or don't do something.*
> *Prevaricating and worrying are a waste*
> *of time and energy.*

THE CAPABLE DIRECTOR
AND THE VIRGINIA CREEPER

The Capable Director was feeling very frustrated. She had set-out a clear plan, built a strong team and gained board approval and a budget. Yet nothing was going as she expected. A succession of executives, some not even connected with her project, popped up to quiz her and her team on the plan, or suggest how things should be different.

The Capable Director decided to share her frustrations with her Wise CEO. She secretly hoped he would just instruct everyone to stop interfering, since it was a great plan.

The Wise CEO listened carefully to her story and then asked her permission to recount a story of his own. The Capable Director nodded, she was a little confused.

'I recently had to cut down several Virginia creepers that had grown from my garden up and over the garden wall which bounds the old church,' the Wise CEO said. 'I did it because this was the ideal place to grow fruit in my garden, since it would be protected by the wall. And everyone would enjoy the fruit.

'I was walking to the church one day when I met one of

my neighbours. She seemed very agitated and I asked her why. She said she was greatly concerned by my actions in cutting down the creeper as she, and others, enjoyed looking at it. So much so, in fact, she was going to mention it to the church committee.'

'What did you say?' asked the Capable Director.

'I agreed that, yes, it was attractive, but then I explained that my fruit trees will be attractive too,' the Wise CEO said quietly.

The Capable Director smiled a knowing smile and continued with her plan.

Many people will have a point of view.
But that doesn't mean you need to change your course.

THE DECISIVE CEO
AND THE INCLUSIVE CEO

When the new Decisive CEO took over, the Mover transport business was a mess: it had slowing growth, huge borrowings and lots of staff unrest. But the Decisive CEO was recruited for her intelligence, clear focus and steely determination. She had a plan and nobody was going to stop her implementing it. Ruthless and forensic in her thinking, she saw to it that she won every argument.

Gradually, the Decisive CEO transformed the business, even though there were many casualties along the way and a growing army of disaffected staff who didn't like her non-inclusive style.

Eventually, after many successful years, the board and management team of Mover became so tired and frustrated by her approach that she was fired.

'We need someone different in style,' said the Mover Chairman. 'Someone who will bring the team together and involve them.'

Everyone agreed. The newly appointed Inclusive CEO was bright and intelligent but ready to hear ideas. Everyone at

Mover was listened to and the contrast with the Decisive CEO couldn't be greater.

Yet, the Inclusive CEO had a habit of reflecting on what he had heard for days and even weeks. He'd take more soundings and involve more people.

Over time, the Mover team became frustrated at the amount of time it took to make a decision. Without a firm view from the top, divisions grew, as did public expressions of frustration about a lack of a clear direction and vision at Mover. Team members started to set their own plans and direction.

After a few years, the board agreed the Inclusive CEO had to go and be replaced by someone with a more decisive approach!

> *No single management style is perfect.*
> *Whether single-minded or team-focused,*
> *be aware of the flaws and compensate.*

THE DETERMINED CHAIRMAN AND THE BOARD PAPERS

The Chairman was determined that he and the non executive board members would do an effective job. He wanted to hold the CEO and her team to account and to be seen to be doing so at marketing giant Flogem.

'I believe we need far more detailed information in papers presented to the board,' boomed the Determined Chairman. 'We need to know what we are dealing with.'

The CEO agreed to the request and papers duly carried more detail. This also meant they got longer and longer. And so did the board meetings!

Still determined to make his mark, the Chairman requested that the briefings were couched in more palatable language to help the non-executive directors understand which bits of information were most pertinent to the debate.

The CEO agreed and even more detail was added around key points. The papers got even longer. And so did the meetings!

Soon the board members began to mutter about the length and detail of the meetings. 'I have had a rethink,' announced the Determined Chairman. 'There is now too much information and reading. Could we cut the papers down to, say, two sides, with just a summary and proposal. If we do that, I think we will have more free-flowing debates.'

The CEO scratched her head.

'So you now want less information, so you can ask questions and make statements unencumbered by the facts?' she asked.

> *Too much information is*
> *as unhelpful as too little!*

THE ANGRY MANAGERS
AND THE WASTED OPPORTUNITY

It was a swelteringly hot day and the shouting in the board-room could be heard through the open windows in the street below. For months the two senior managers at Bustup had clashed over whether to do a deal to buy another company and now it had all come to a head.

'It will wreck our business, and I'm against doing it,' screamed the Adverse Manager.

'We will be wrecked if we don't, which is why we should do it,' yelled back the Favourable Manager.

'It's a distraction from what we do now,' came the reply.

'It will help us do what we do now,' was the retort.

'If you had my management consulting background you would know this was a huge risk,' hissed the Adverse Manager.

'If you had my practical experience you wouldn't be so dumb,' scoffed the Favourable Manager.

And so the insults flew in the heat of the day. They seemed to being getting ever stronger and more personal and completely drowned out what others had to say. The meeting Chair tried to intervene, but felt hopeless to stop the warring.

'If we can't all agree, we can't move forward,' exclaimed the overwhelmed Chair finally, much to the frustration of the Favourable Manager and the delight of the Adverse Manager.

No one ever found out whether this was the right decision or not.

It is often more helpful and constructive
to understand why *people hold the views they do,*
than the views themselves.

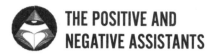

THE POSITIVE AND NEGATIVE ASSISTANTS

There were two young assistants who were recruited to Best Foot Adventure Holidays, each with very different characters. One was bright and positive, the other cynical and negative. While the Positive Assistant always saw challenges and problems as part of the job and found joy in solving them, the Negative Assistant just moaned that things weren't perfect. He swore that if others got things right, his life would be so much easier.

One day it was announced that the Positive Assistant was to be promoted. The Negative Assistant was not much impressed and took it as yet another sign that things were just never destined to go well for him.

Time after time the same thing happened. The Negative Assistant looked on in mute misery as others rose above him. The pattern lasted right up until the Negative Assistant reached retirement age, still barely above the level where he had started.

On his last day, his manager, who had once been his old colleague the Positive Assistant, asked him if there is anything he would have changed about his time working for the business.

Reflecting hard, the Negative Assistant said: 'I wish I had chosen to be happier!'

Each day we decide
whether or not to be happy

THE HEEDFUL TRAINEE
AND THE WATER COOLER

Long ago, at the beginning of his career at Blossom Inc., the Heedful Trainee made it his priority to be successful and well liked by the staff. The Heedful Trainee resolved to listen to every complaint, no matter how small, and promised himself that when he was able he would solve their concerns.

In those days, staff only ever talked about one thing: the water cooler! It had been broken forever! 'Surely it wouldn't be hard to fix it!' the staff complained. 'Why will no one listen to us?'

The Heedful Trainee listened. And so, on the very day the Heedful Trainee finally became a manager at Blossom Inc., he fixed the water cooler.

How the staff sang his praises! 'Finally, someone in management cares about us!'

The Heedful Trainee, who was now a Heedful Manager, thought he had done his job well.

So he was utterly baffled when the Managing Director showed up at his office at the end of the day.

'Did you think I didn't know the water cooler was

broken?' asked the Managing Director. 'Do you think I don't care about my staff? Or that we didn't have the money to fix the water cooler?'

'Of course not!' replied the Heedful Manager. 'I thought a manager's job was to give his staff what they want!'

The Managing Director sighed.

'You are no longer just a trainee, but you still have much to learn,' he said. 'With the watercooler mended, what will the staff complain about now?'

People will always complain about something.
Think about what you would like it to be.

CHAPTER THIRTEEN

Dealing with the competition

THE POACHED EXECUTIVE AND THE LONG TRIP

Colossus had been the biggest and best business in its sector for many years. One day though, Mouse, a smaller, nimbler rival, began to snap at its heels.

'I'm fed-up with everyone telling me how clever they are,' the Colossus Chairman fumed to his board. 'I've got a plan though. I am going to recruit one of Mouse's young, ambitious executives. That way we will get their secrets, slow them up and show everyone we are the biggest and the best.'

It wasn't long before they did a deal to recruit the Poached Executive. And why wouldn't he accept? They offered him an extraordinary package to join Collossus.

However, when the Poached Executive told his company he was leaving, they insisted he work his six months notice, as per his contract. This made the Collossus Chairman even more cross.

He got straight on the phone to complain to the boss of Mouse.

'You can't possibly want this chap to keep working for you,' he exploded. 'He wants to join us. Besides, he will see all your secrets. We always let our departing executives go straight away. Why won't you do that?'

But the Poached Executive's boss knew he could cause his bigger rival a headache.

'Thank you for your concern,' he began. 'Obviously we can't remove what he already has in his head. However, we have some important work abroad that he can do for the next six months. That will keep him away from sensitive company information.'

The Poached Executive was duly sent to work abroad and the Mouse boss appointed an internal candidate to fill his former role with immediate effect.

The smaller company sailed on while Colossus had to wait half a year for their man, by which time he had no up-to-date intelligence on their rival.

Never underestimate your competition.

Big is not always the best.

THE GREEN-EYED BOSS AND
THE CHRISTMAS SURVIVAL KIT

Christmas is always a busy time for gift businesses, but a huge amount of planning and preparation goes on beforehand. One year, the rivalry between two gift businesses peaked, just before they entered their busiest period. The Green-Eyed Boss at Gifthive had absolutely had it up to the back teeth with his rival, the Always Calm Boss of GiftCo. The Always Calm Boss had better managers, better staff, better products and prices, better marketing and was held in higher regard. The Green-Eyed Boss, a gritty trader, was sick and tired of hearing about his rival's success and keen to get the better of them.

I know, thought the Green-Eyed Boss, *I will get GiftCo's top managers to come and work for me. That way I will improve my business and harm theirs in the all-important Christmas trading period.*

So, that is what the Green-Eyed Boss asked his HR Director to arrange. Managers at GiftCo were telephoned with tempting offers to switch sides.

The Calm Boss at GiftCo, having heard what was happening, decided to teach the Green-Eyed Boss a lesson. During the run-up to Christmas trading, GiftCo always sent its managers a survival kit to get through the busy period. It was a fun package and came with a note from the Calm Boss thanking everyone in advance for their hard work over the busy Christmas peak.

This year, keen to get his own back, the Calm Boss also sent survival kits to all Gifthive's managers, wishing them well. On the note accompanying it was a special telephone number for the Gifthive manager to call if they wanted a better job. So impressed were the Gifthive staff with the Christmas pack and the care the rival's managers received, dozens applied to work at GiftCo. In fact, ten times as many good managers left Gifthive as had been recruited in the first instance from GiftCo.

Be careful not to provoke a much
bigger and stronger competitor.

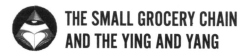

THE SMALL GROCERY CHAIN
AND THE YING AND YANG

While the Big Supermarkets focused on lowering prices, the Small Grocery Chain focused on improving quality and innovation. As a result, the Small Grocery Chain grew more quickly than the others.

After a time, the Big Supermarkets noticed the Small Grocery Chain was growing fast and decided to focus more on quality and innovation. The Big Supermarkets hired celebrity chefs, introduced new, more expensive ranges and started to shout about their improving quality in adverts.

The Small Grocery Chain, seeing the move, started to focus on improving their value by introducing a new range of less expensive products, dropping their prices and increasing promotions. As a result, customers started to shop there more.

The Big Supermarkets noticed how price competitive the Small Grocery Chain was becoming and that their sales were growing. They decided to cut the quality of what they sold and reduce staffing. And so the Smaller Grocery Chain began to focus once again on quality!

*The most successful and proven
business strategy is to do the opposite of what
your competitors are doing.*

THE BITTER BOSS AND THE CHOCOLATELESS CHOCOLATE CAKE

For many years, Cakealicious was *the* place to go to buy a special cake. It made cakes in all shapes and sizes, for christenings, weddings, birthdays and celebrations. People talked in hushed tones about the joy of opening a Cakealicious box to behold the fine cake inside. They just knew they were going to experience a fabulous taste sensation.

And the best seller of all? The double chocolate gateau.

Over the years, tastes and budgets changed. Other shops began to offer celebration cakes in nice boxes and they priced them cheaper too. But people always returned to Cakealicious when they wanted a real treat.

Fearful of losing market share, the boss at Cakealicious became bitter. He called his team around him and demanded that they find a way to make more money on what they sold to make their profits increase.

'We need to reduce the price of our products by 5 per cent each year, for the next five years, to give our customers better value,' the Bitter Boss told them.

There were gulps all round, then nods of agreement in the

room. The chief cake buyer thought about the challenge and decided to add a little less chocolate to the best-selling birthday cake. *No one will notice,* she thought. And she was right.

The packaging still looked attractive and people still bought the cake. This went on for the next few years and still no one noticed.

The Bitter Boss at Cakealicious was still fearful of the competition though. He demanded even tougher targets. Charged with finding new ways to make cost savings, the chief cake buyer used chocolate extract and colouring, rather than real chocolate. Nobody noticed the change in the ingredients listed on the box and people still bought the celebration cakes with joy and anticipation in their hearts.

Then, ever so gradually, customers started to realise that rival chocolate cakes were quite a lot nicer and only slightly more expensive. Sales began to fall and the chief cake buyer was fired. The Bitter Boss of Cakealicious blamed his fussy customers for wanting even more of a bargain. He started to demand ever-more stringent cuts.

To the customer, value isn't just low prices.
It is a combination of quality and price.

THE PLEASANT PROPRIETORS AND THE SWITCHED LEASES

The Pleasant Proprietors had run the Sew and Sew chain for thirty years. They opened small haberdashery shops in the centre of busy market towns and served their communities with bric-a-brac and sewing essentials. They made sure to get to know their customers and were always happy to offer advice, or simply a kindly ear.

One day, the Pleasant Proprietors were shocked to hear that the lease on their original shop had been abruptly terminated. The landlord called and said it would not be renewed.

It transpired that a rival chain, Thimbler, had persuaded the landlord to switch to them by promising to pay a much higher rent.

Alarmed, the Pleasant Proprietors contacted the Thimbler boss to ask if he intended to bid for the leases of any of their other shops.

'No, no, of course not!' he soothed. 'There must have been a misunderstanding.'

But he was lying. Not long afterwards, the Pleasant Proprietors received first one call and then another from landlords terminating their other leases. It transpired that these landlords had been approached by Thimble too.

The Pleasant Proprietors realised that their competitor could not be trusted and decided to teach them a lesson. First, they contacted all the competitor's landlords to say they were interested in taking Thimbler's sites when its leases were due for renewal. By doing so they knew they'd be increasing their competitor's costs in the future, because the landlords would bank on a bidding war for their shops.

The Pleasant Proprietors then quickly opened another Sew and Sew shop in the small market town while Thimbler was still working on converting their old shop. When the competitor finally opened it had far fewer customers than it had planned for. Having committed to a high rent, Thimbler began to struggle.

When words and actions don't match,
it's actions that speak louder than words.

THE CHIC AND CHICHI CEOS
AND THE VERY PUBLIC SPAT

There were once two fashion brands, Fashion East and Fashion West, and they loathed each other with a passion. Each had, at one time, been the biggest names in their industry and both were keen to rise again to take the top slot. The Chic CEO at Fashion West was convinced that Fashion East had muddied the waters by selling its wares too cheaply. Fashion East's Chichi CEO was equally certain the Fashion West had ruined it for everyone by charging too much for its clothes.

Finally, the constant side-swiping escalated into an all-out war of words. Fashion East kicked off the spring season with a provocative series of adverts declaring that its clothes were a bargain.

The furious Chic CEO at Fashion West fired back a full-page salvo declaring Fashion East was not a bargain, it was 'just cheap'.

Not to be outdone, the Chichi CEO came right back with her own retort, questioning the quality and value for money money of her rival's brand.

The press lapped up the fight as the Chic and Chichi CEOs

became more and more determined to knock each other off their perches.

Eventually Fashion East took Fashion West to court and asked the judge to endorse their case. All this time the business's customers had looked on, dismayed at the arguing. Many didn't like the spectacle of the two brands involved in such a bitter public dispute and shopped elsewhere, to the benefit of the others in the market.

Meanwhile, the court case and the war of words dragged on.

Don't lose sight of what it is you do.
When consumed with moral indignation it
is easy to lose track of how customers
might view things.

THE CIRCUMSPECT CONSULTANT AND THE LUXURY CAR MAKER

Sales were flying when the new CEO took over at the helm of the luxury car business. He was keen to make his mark and his first thought was that a focus on tighter cost control would boost profits.

Like many new CEOs, he brought in a consultant to advise him. Mind you, he gave him quite a clear steer on the way he was thinking!

The Circumspect Consultant met the board and then toured the factory in order to prepare his report. In the first large room he came across four highly qualified chemists who were working on what the car should smell like when the owner climbed into their prized possession. Wafts of leather, wood and vanilla scents filled the air.

The Circumspect Consultant mused: *There is an obvious way to save some money here.*

In the next room a large group of P.h.D-educated engineers were working on the 'thud' the door should make when it was closed, to reassure the owner on the quality of build.

More saving, thought the Circumspect Consultant.

The next room had highly trained physiotherapists looking at the most comfortable and efficient driving positions.

And so it went on through every process, from the overall design to the engine and brakes and windscreens. There was an overwhelming array of skilled professionals looking to improve every detail of the luxury car.

The Circumspect Consultant returned to meet the board at the end of the trip. The CEO, expecting confirmation of his plan to pare down on costs, was surprised to hear the verdict of the Circumspect Consultant.

'You make the most prestigious cars in the world. They are the ultimate driving machines. Everybody who works here is dedicated to that single goal. That gives you a competitive advantage you should never lose.'

The Circumspect Consultant didn't win the contract to help lower costs but the car company went from strength to strength.

Don't throw away your competitive
advantage for short-term gain.

CHAPTER FOURTEEN

Growing a business

THE STEADY MANAGER
AND THE BIG JOB OFFER

The Steady Manager had worked at Get Active leisure firm for many years. She enjoyed the respect of the staff and directors alike and knew exactly what the company's customers wanted.

The Steady Manager was constantly busy making lots of small changes. Each year she would shrink or grow Get Active's product ranges, depending upon what her customers wanted. She'd carefully introduce new services and retrain the team in any new skills required. Get Active's growth was consistent.

Get Active's competitors looked on with envy as year after year their rival outpaced them.

'We must get the very best managers to beat Get Active,' they declared. 'We'll pay anything!'

And so they did. With each new manager came new reviews, new strategies and new teams. Yet, even with so much change, they continued to have indifferent results.

In desperation one of Get Active's chief rivals tried to poach the Steady Manager.

'Will you join us?' the boss of the rival firm asked

the Steady Manager. 'We will pay you as much as you would like.'

'I am afraid you would be disappointed in me and so my answer is no,' replied the Steady Manager.

'But why?' asked the boss.

'I believe that 100 times 1 per cent of improvements is better than 1 times 100 per cent improvement,' the Steady Manager replied. 'That takes time and patience. It's also something you don't have, which you have amply demonstrated through your constant hiring and firing.'

Revolutions are risky and rarely succeed.
Evolution is often better for long-term growth.

THE COMPANY SPY AND THE ROTATING BUYERS

The Linked chain store had long been frustrated by Connected, a rival that seemed to out-do it at every turn. Finally the bosses had had enough. They decided to send in one of their own buyers as a Company Spy.

When the Company Spy arrived at Connected, the buying team seemed very happy and friendly. The Company Spy was a little confused by the way they worked though. It seemed completely different from his real job. He mentioned it to his new colleague.

'What happened at your old job?' the colleague asked the Company Spy.

'Well, we never stuck around in one department for long,' the Company Spy explained. 'My bosses were worried that if buyers bought the same goods for too long, they would build a relationship with suppliers that was too close. They thought that that would make us too lenient in our negotiations. To keep everyone on their toes, Linked buyers were constantly rotated.'

'Things are different here,' the Connected colleague

explained. 'Here you can buy your category for as long as you wish. We like to build long and deep relationships with our suppliers. That way they always come to us first with new products and ideas. We also pay them fairly, so that when we need their help we get it. That is how we always stay one step ahead of the competition and enjoy our work.'

The Company Spy was shocked, but inspired. He immediately quit his job and began to work for Connected for real!

Building long and consistent
relationships will pay dividends.

THE EMPIRE-BUILDING EXECUTIVE AND THE PROPERTY PORTFOLIO

For many years there were three shops at the top of their game. They always competed hard against one another, but no one ever seemed to come out far ahead of their rivals. They were, however, streets ahead of the competition.

One day, the Chief Executive of one of the shops decided to settle the rivalry once and for all. He recruited a new executive and told him to spare no expense.

'I want to be the undisputed biggest,' he declared. 'Don't get bogged down worrying about profits. Just focus on sales growth, market share and cashflow.'

'Then it is property that you need to invest in,' confirmed the Empire-Building Executive.

'Brilliant,' declared the chief executive. 'Buy, buy, buy. I'll make sure you get big bonuses if you open lots of new space.'

And so the Empire-Building Executive bought big shops, little shops, chains of shops and bits of other shops. He bought any space he could find and sometimes he would even pay twice as much as others were willing to pay, just to hit his bonus target.

Just as the CEO wanted, sales grew and so did market share. Plus cash from operations increased. Of course, profits hardly budged, but no one said anything because the chain had at last shown its two rivals a clean pair of heels.

One day, there was a dreadful recession. Property prices slumped and suddenly the expensive new shops were a burden. The company was forced to write off hundreds of millions of pounds worth of assets since the shops were no longer worth what had been paid for them.

The Empire-Building Executive quietly moved on to another business to continue his stellar career.

Buying assets in a rush to grow
sales will always end in tears.

THE ENTHUSIASTIC EXECUTIVE AND THE SHRINKING BABY

Buy Buy Fresh was a thriving firm selling low-cost fresh food to families. The Enthusiastic Executive was very happy to join Buy Buy Fresh because she was full of great ideas.

'Why don't we start selling baby care items too,' she said, bubbling over with what she might do. 'We have lots of young families shopping with us already. We could buy an online baby business and also sell the products in our stores too. Maybe one day we might even build it up into a standalone shop business.'

The Buy Buy Fresh bosses admired the Enthusiastic Executive and all her great new concepts. They let her progress the idea and then, when the new baby care package seemed to be going OK, they gave the nod to the next stage of the expansion.

The Enthusiastic Executive raced off and found some large shops on the edge of a number of market towns.

'These will be great for young families,' she glowed. 'We will be *the* out-of-town destination for baby products.'

The sale price for these units was higher than Buy Buy Fresh expected, but buoyed by the Enthusiastic Executive's sales pitch, the company backed the expansion.

Frustratingly, young families did not flock to the new baby store. They weren't so keen to travel to out-of-town sites and didn't see the point of only going there for baby goods. Not to be put off, the Enthusiastic Executive requested that some of Buy Buy Fresh's best people were seconded to the baby stores to turn them around.

Despite the talented executives' best efforts they still couldn't grow sales by enough to cover their costs. Eventually Buy Buy Fresh had to sell the baby care business at an enormous loss. Millions of pounds, that could have been spent on making the food business better, had been wasted and all that time Buy Buy Fresh's main business lost ground.

> *If you move from what you are good at,*
> *make sure you have the skills, time and*
> *money to make it work.*

THE BOLD BOSS AND THE BIG EXPANSION

The Bold Boss ran a large chain of supermarkets called Shopzilla. Keen to make his mark, the Bold Boss instigated a plan to takeover a competitor with similar stores, doubling the size of Shopzilla overnight.

Shareholders were delighted.

To keep on growing, the Bold Boss decided to sell clothes and hardware alongside the groceries traditionally sold by Shopzilla.

Sales soared, everyone was pleased. But, of course, there was always room for improvement.

'I know, we'll build Mini Shopzillas in towns with no space for the big version,' declared the Bold Boss.

That's exactly what they did and the plaudits grew.

Shopzilla was now running out of room in its home territory, so the Bold Boss took the brand overseas. He agreed to franchise the Shopzilla name to local companies, because he reasoned locals would know better how local customers shopped. It was a runaway success!

Emboldened, the Bold Boss agreed a joint 50:50 venture

with an overseas retailer. Then, when that worked like a dream, he took the next logical step and went it alone.

Shopzilla built their own supermarkets abroad on an entirely new continent, taking all the lessons they had gained elsewhere and developing a brand-new cutting edge offer with a new name. Billions of pounds were invested in building a supply base, infrastructure and shops.

'We can do anything!' declared the Bold Manager.

Except they couldn't. Competitors worked hard to make life difficult and customers didn't quickly warm to Shopzilla's revolutionary new approach and, after the losses kept growing, the business was sold for a fraction of the price it cost to build. The failure weighed heavily with investors and management and knocked the successful business from its stride.

Over-confidence often leads to failure.

THE RELIABLE FAMILY AND THE FAST FEET BUSINESS

The BootCo shoe shop had been owned and run by the Reliable Family for one hundred years. Over time the Reliable Family had kitted out innumerable children with their school shoes and then measured and cared for the feet of each successive generation. The Reliable Family prided themselves on having the best designs, the highest standards of service and well-appointed shops.

Even after all these years, BootCo still only had a dozen shops. The Reliable Family were not prepared to open a new one unless they had a manager and staff available who understood how they worked and the high level of customer service they aspired to.

'It's monastic growth,' the present generation's boss liked to joke.

Some clever money men looked at BootCo and observed how slow and fragmented the shoe market was.

'We can do much better than that,' they scoffed.

Knowing how cheap money was to borrow, they hatched a plan to quickly build a huge shoe empire called Fleet of Foot.

They intended to buy lots and lots of small shoe shop chains and put them together.

They borrowed and bought and borrowed and bought until it seemed like every week the board were agreeing a new deal to buy a Fleet of Foot branch. New staff barely had time to be trained before they were managing a new shop.

But BootCo's customers continued to flock to them for their expert advice and each time they opened a new shop with existing trained staff they took Fleet of Foot's trade. They might not have been the biggest but they were certainly regarded as the best.

Sustained success takes patience.

THE FOOLHARDY PRINTER AND THE BIG PROMOTION

The Foolhardy Printer had great plans for the future of his small printing company Printamondo. He was certain that one day it would be a huge and successful business with contracts all over the globe.

So, the moment the opportunity arose, the Foolhardy Printer put in a bid for an enormous job; the printing of two million money-off vouchers for a large holiday company's Easter promotion.

The Foolhardy Printer ensured Printamondo came in with the lowest price by far and reassured the holiday company that his firm could meet the tight deadline. To his joy, he won the contract.

Yet, Printamondo had never managed an order of this scale before. The business was hopelessly out of its depth. It could only dribble out the direct-mail vouchers in batches. Many customers did not receive their vouchers until after the Easter deadline.

The holiday company refused to pay the bill and vowed never to use Printamondo again. They even spread the word elsewhere. As a result of the debacle, the Foolhardy Printer had to close his business.

> *Do not make promises unless you*
> *are confident you can keep them.*

THE FAR-SIGHTED MANAGING DIRECTOR WHO CARED FOR CUSTOMERS

The Chain Store had a mantra: Never give away margin.

The idea was to take full advantage of its customers. As a result, each year prices went up and customer numbers fell. The business didn't really grow, but the Chain Store founders were happy enough.

Yet, when the market became tougher, the company's uncompetitive pricing saw many more customers than normal leave. It was time to act.

The new, Far-Sighted Managing Director had a plan. There would be new product launches each spring and Chain Store would offer discounts each autumn to attract more customers.

Many in Chain Store's old guard shook their heads at this policy, but customers welcomed it. They returned to Chain Store and lapped up the new and unique products.

There were further murmurings when the Far-Sighted Managing Director cut prices to match the price of similar products elsewhere.

'We are giving money away,' some said.

But the Far-Sighted Managing Director stuck to her guns

and explained that if sales increased by 5 per cent, the cost of the reductions would be more than covered. She was right too, and even better, sales grew by 10 per cent.

New services were added, so customers could just go to one Chain Store for all they needed. Some questioned the cost and the extra training required but the Far-Sighted Managing Director was resolute. Sure enough, customer numbers and sales grew.

Finally, the Far-Sighted Managing Director invested the majority of the marketing budget to give more to their current customers with offers and promotions. They were so pleased they told their friends.

The business grew and grew.

Think in the long term. Your success depends on looking after the customers you have.

THE FORTUNE HUNTER AND THE ART OF SELLING

There were once two young entrepreneurs who had market stalls next to each other: the Speculator and the Fortune Hunter.

Both bought white T-shirts from the Far East for one pound and sold them for two. Both sold the same amount every week.

Keen to get ahead, the Speculator dropped the price of his T-shirts to £1.90 and began to sell more than his neighbour. But, instead of following suit, the Fortune Hunter had a cunning plan.

Rather than drop his price to £1.90, which would mean both stallholders made less money, the Fortune Hunter arranged to have a purple rabbit embroidered on the chest of his T-shirts. It cost him just a few pounds to do this.

The Fortune Hunter then put his T-shirts out on his stall with a new sign.

It read: 'Exclusive Purple Rabbit Designer T-Shirts. £10.'

The Purple Rabbit T-shirts became a hit and the Fortune Hunter made lots of profit.

*There are cleverer ways to grow
a business than just cutting prices.*

 THE ENERGETIC ENTREPRENEUR WHO BELIEVED BIGGER IS BETTER

The Energetic Entrepreneur behind Variety Store was unequivocal: 'Bigger is better!' was his mantra.

So, first of all, pack sizes were made bigger to give customers better value. Families lapped it up, but couples and those living alone didn't want larger sizes.

'Now we will make our shops bigger,' announced the Energetic Entrepreneur. 'I want them huge, with every product possible.'

While those who wanted everything in one place approved, those who just wanted to quickly pop in and out found the monster-sized Variety Stores unwieldy.

'Now I want more shops,' declared the Energetic Entrepreneur. 'More than anyone else. We are going to be the biggest and then we can offer the lowest prices. That will make us the best.'

Variety Store bought more and more shops, but as they did so, it became harder and harder to maintain consistently good customer service standards.

Each year there was a national customer poll to decide

which was the best all-round shop. The ever-larger Variety Store never won, or even came close to winning.

> *Bigger isn't better,*
> *only better is better*

THE EXHAUSTED BANKER
AND HAPPY FISHERMAN

An Exhausted Banker arrived at his beautiful Caribbean hotel for a well-earned rest. He looked out over the golden beach and the bright morning sun shinning off the azure sea and noticed the Happy Fisherman pushing his boat out.

How lucky that man is, thought the Exhausted Banker.

The Exhausted Banker watched as the Happy Fisherman returned with his catch at lunchtime and then sell it to the hotel's chef. The fisherman then sat at a small table on the beach and was served one of his own fish and a few beers by the hotel kitchen. After a snooze in the shade the fishermen took his boat out again.

At dusk the Happy Fisherman returned with yet more fish and once again sold them to the hotel's chef. He was then joined by his family and they all sat round the beach table eating and drinking and laughing.

The Exhausted Banker kept watching this routine and as each day passed he felt himself getting more and more envious. Finally he decided to approach the Happy Fisherman with a plan.

The Exhausted Banker told the Happy Fisherman that if the fisherman were to let him invest in his business he could buy a bigger boat, go out further and for longer and supply all the hotels on the island. Soon, the Exhausted Banker went on, the Happy Fisherman would be able to invest in a small fleet of boats, hire a number of crew and supply all the Caribbean islands. With the business then at a certain size it could be floated on the New York Stock Exchange and, with the funds raised, a huge fleet could be purchased. The Happy Fisherman could supply restaurants and hotels on North America's eastern seaboard.

'And what would I do then?' interrupted the Happy Fisherman.

'Well, you could come to an expensive hotel like this one for a vacation. Relax in the sun, fish when you want to and spend the rest of the time with your family.'

The Happy Fisherman smiled and replied: 'No, thank you. That is the life I have already!'

Make grand plans, by all means,
but check first if you already have all that you desire.

CHAPTER FIFTEEN

Costly mistakes
and watching your back

THE CANNY CHEESE SELLER
AND THE SUPERMARKET

The Canny Cheese Seller had built-up a great little business. He and his family travelled to France, bought up a selection of fabulous exotic cheeses, then returned home, repackaged them and then sold them on to a large supermarket chain.

The Supermarket Cheese Buyer liked the arrangement with the Canny Cheese Seller. He clearly knew his cheeses and seemed to be quite content to do all the leg-work. All the Supermarket Cheese Buyer had to do was taste the produce, agree quantities and pay the agreed price.

When the Supermarket Cheese Buyer retired he commended the Canny Cheese Seller's company to his successor. However, the New Supermarket Cheese Buyer had misgivings. She was concerned that similar cheeses appeared to cost much less at other supermarkets.

The retiring buyer explained it the way the Canny Cheese Seller had presented the discrepancy to him.

'This is because those other supermarkets are much larger businesses and buy much more cheese, so they can negotiate lower prices,' he said confidently.

The New Supermarket Cheese Buyer wasn't convinced and asked the finance team to check the Canny Cheese Seller's accounts. She was horrified to discover that the specialist French producers actually made so little cheese that it wasn't possible for the rival supermarkets to be negotiating cheaper prices for large orders, as the retiring buyer had suggested. In reality, the Canny Cheese Buyer was just charging a lot of money to select, transport and pack the cheese and the retiring buyer had never bothered to delve more deeply into the situation.

The New Supermarket Cheese Buyer ended the Canny Cheese Seller's contract and the supermarket started dealing directly with the producers. Prices dropped significantly.

> *There is always someone waiting*
> *to take advantage of lazy actions.*

THE COST-CUTTER, THE CAPABLE CHAIRMAN AND THE YACHT RACE

There were once two company chairmen who were the bitterest of enemies. One chairman had worked himself up from the shop floor, building his reputation through ruthless cost cutting. The Cost-Cutting Chairman loathed his rival, the Capable Chairman, because he had simply inherited a business. He'd never accept that, although he had been born into advantage, the Capable Chairman also had an intuitive flair for business. The Capable Chairman, for his part, did his best to ignore the constant snide comments coming from his competitor.

One day, the two men were invited by a mutual supplier to participate in a week-long yacht race. Both the chairmen initially accepted, but then the Cost-Cutting Chairman saw his rival was also going along and saw his chance. He declined the offer at the last moment and waited patiently for his adversary to be on the high seas, hundreds of miles away.

As soon as he was certain that the Capable Chairman was engaged in the yacht race, the Cost-Cutting Chairman launched a hostile takeover for his rival's company. He told shareholders that his rival was a privileged playboy, uninterested in driving cost savings.

'He prefers to disappear for a week on a luxury yacht, rather than concentrate on protecting your investment,' he crowed.

The Capable Chairman rushed back to London as soon as he heard what had happened, but it was too late. The damage had been done and he lost the business.

Understand how your rivals
could exploit your perceived flaws.

THE SHARP SHOPKEEPERS
AND THE SHRINKING PACK SIZE

The Sharp Shopkeepers at the MadBargain discount store chain were very pleased with their sales success. Customers flocked to their shops because they believed they were getting goods at a much better value than anywhere else. They loved the fact that they could buy brand-name goods at under a pound.

The Sharp Shopkeepers constantly fought to keep their prices down. But, one day, they had a very difficult meeting with one of their suppliers. The supplier, who sold them biscuits, explained that costs had gone up and therefore prices would have to increase.

The Sharp Shopkeepers were perplexed. If they sold the biscuits at the price the supplier demanded, customers would walk away. They expected to buy everything for under a pound.

'What if the packs you sell us have one fewer biscuit than the ones you sell elsewhere?' suggested one of the Sharp Shopkeepers to the supplier. 'Could you then give us the same price as before?'

The supplier thought about it and nodded.

The customers didn't notice and they still thought they

were getting a great deal at MadBargains. Each year, the supplier and the Sharp Shopkeepers had the same conversation and each year pack sizes slowly shrank as either the number of biscuits, or size of biscuit, reduced. MadBargains kept its prices below a pound throughout.

You get what you pay for.

THE COCKY CHIEF EXECUTIVE AND THE HELICOPTER

The Cocky Chief Executive was always in a hurry and thought himself very grand. While he had done an excellent job in building his business, he had little time for small talk.

'Time is money,' he was often heard saying.

One day, he had a very busy schedule of factory visits and had to be here, there and everywhere. He huffed and puffed about how precious his time was and asked his PA to sort out a helicopter to whizz him around quickly.

'But what will the workers think?' asked his PA.

'Who cares, they are simple people doing simple jobs,' replied the Cocky Chief Executive. 'Their jobs don't keep them away from home. They don't have the responsibility I have.'

'Well, shouldn't you at least explain why you are using the helicopter?' pressed the PA. 'You know, so you can visit more factories in a day?'

'I don't need to answer to the factory workers,' said the Cocky Chief Executive indignantly. 'If it wasn't for me they wouldn't have jobs.'

The PA reluctantly booked the helicopter and arranged for

it to land at each factory. The sight of it arriving caused quite a stir amongst the workers who came out to watch. But, as was his way, the Cocky Chief Executive ignored them. There was no smile, no hello and no handshake as he went to see the factory manager. He ignored the workers completely, only talking to the manager. He didn't say goodbye or well done as he left but simply headed for his waiting helicopter and off he flew. He repeated the same behaviour at all the factories he visited that day.

The Cocky Chief Executive's actions were not well received by the workers and they were quick to comment on how ignorant the Cocky Chief Executive had been and how brash. The workers felt undervalued and wanted redress. If he can travel by helicopter we deserve more money, they observed. The Chairman heard and was not amused. He sacked the Cocky Chief Executive despite his previous successes.

> *Don't forget what makes a business tick –*
> *its people. Never lose sight of the everyday.*

THE SMILING PA AND THE JOB APPLICANTS

It was the day of the big interview for the most sought-after job in the company. One by one, the candidates trooped into the office building.

They were met by the Managing Director's Smiling PA who was waiting in reception to take them to the boardroom for interview.

The Smiling PA asked each of them the same questions.

'Where have you come from?

'How was the journey?

'Have you had a holiday this year?'

And finally, on arriving at the board anteroom, she asked if they would like a hot drink while they waited.

After all the applicants had all been interviewed, the Managing Director called the Smiling PA to the boardroom.

'I am thinking of offering the job to so-and-so,' she said. 'What do you think?'

'Not for me,' replied the PA with a firm shake of her head. 'When I asked him a question, he could barely be bothered to look at me, or answer. The only thing he asked me was whether you were in a good mood. And he didn't say please or thank you when I got him a drink.'

'Thank you,' said the Managing Director. She then went on to offer the job to someone who had engaged professionally with the Smiling PA.

Everybody matters.

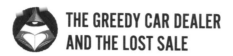

THE GREEDY CAR DEALER
AND THE LOST SALE

The Prospective Car Buyer walked into his local car showroom intent on buying a new car. The Greedy Car Dealer sidled up to him and offered him a test drive.

The Prospective Car Buyer was impressed.

'What is your best price?' he asked after the drive.

'I suppose I could give you a small discount, but this really, really is the lowest I can go,' said the Greedy Car Dealer and named a price.

The Prospective Car Buyer thanked him and said he would think about it.

But then he found a much lower price from a dealer 200 miles away from home and travelled by train to buy the new car.

A few days later the Greedy Car Dealer phoned to see if the Prospective Car Buyer was still interested. He was furious to find he had gone elsewhere.

'But why didn't you come back to me and say you had found a lower price?' he fumed. 'I would have matched it.'

'I asked you what your best price was,' the Prospective

Car Buyer said. 'And you told me it was really, really the lowest you could go. You didn't suggest you would think again.'

Always give yourself the
chance to have a second shot.

THE EXPERIENCED RETAIL MANAGER WHO LOVED HIS OLD JOB

The Experienced Retail Manager had yearned to run a big retail business all his life. When he heard the struggling store chain FanFare was looking for a new boss, he leaped at the opportunity.

The Experienced Retail Manager managed to impress the recruitment board with his encyclopaedic knowledge of retail and got the job.

The first thing the Experienced Retail Manager did when he arrived at FanFare was sack the retail manager. After all, he knew he could do a much better job and he loved being in charge of retail. He immediately immersed himself in all the things he knew so much about, such as pay costs, shrinkage, customer service and presentation – in fact, all the things great retail managers focus on. Things in the retail division got better and everyone agreed what a great retail man he was.

However, the Experienced Retail Manager paid little attention to anything else, such as finance, buying, strategy, product development and the supply chain. Each department that had nothing directly to do with retail began to suffer hugely with no thought, attention or direction put into them. Neglecting just one of them would have been damaging, but ignoring them all was downright catastrophic. Soon the struggling business was struggling even more and the Experienced Retail Manager was asked to leave.

> *It is foolish to keep doing your old job*
> *if you have been hired to do another.*

THE CONSULTANCY VETERAN AND THE NEW APPROACH

The Trade Up! retail business was always known for its innovation and flair. Successive owners had built upon the legacy laid down by Trade Up! creatives. But the Trade Up! chain always had excellent cost control too. In tough times, the business did even better relatively to its competitors. Instead of blindly cutting costs, it made sure it's overall product range was even more fresh and eye-catching.

Everyone was curious about the new choice of boss. The Consultancy Veteran had been classically trained at business school. His main focus was on productivity and efficiency, rather than creativity. When tough times came, as they always do, the Consultancy Veteran's answer was to introduce even more efficiency, not differentiation. He centralised, cut and invested in technology to reduce costs, but didn't give much thought to customers and the product range. In fact, to everyone's shock, the Consultancy Veteran even *reduced* the budget for innovation and design.

Year by year Trade Up! became less appealing to customers. Less was spent on new designs and people could no longer find the styles they loved. To see off the worst, the Consultancy Veteran slashed costs still further, but with fewer customers TradeUp! never recovered to its former glory.

You cannot cut your way to business growth.
It can only be done by pleasing the customer
in good times and bad.

THE DETERMINED FACTORY MANAGER AND THE BISCUIT DEAL

The new Bix biscuit factory was much bigger and more efficient than the old one. In fact, it was so efficient, it wasn't even working to full capacity.

'If only we could fill that spare capacity,' thought the Determined Factory Manager. 'That would make us very profitable indeed.'

One day, a discount retailer came to see the Determined Factory Manager and said he would order enough to fill the extra capacity. However, he added, he would need to pay a little less for each pack of biscuits, since he'd be selling them for less.

The Determined Factory Manager calculated that, apart from the small amount of extra labour needed to run the machines a little longer, plus the extra ingredients and packaging, all the other costs, such as power, rent, rates, paying back the loans on the building and machines, were covered by the other customers. If he worked with the discount retailer he could make a little extra profit. He agreed the deal.

The discounter sold his biscuits at a lot less than they could be bought from elsewhere, greatly helped by the fact that he had a lower cost price. It didn't take long before customers found out and soon everyone started buying the biscuits from the discounter and stopped buying elsewhere. The discounter ordered more biscuits at the lower price and the other supermarkets ordered far less at the higher price.

Soon half the production capacity of the larger Bix factory was going on the cheaper priced biscuits and the company's profit crumbled.

Stretching for a little more can sometimes cost much more than you think.

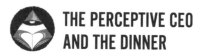

THE PERCEPTIVE CEO AND THE DINNER

The Perceptive CEO of BigCo asked his assistant to book a hotel for a meeting and dinner with his top managers. The assistant called their local hotel and explained that the CEO of BigCo was getting his senior team together for a meeting and dinner and would very much like to hold it at the hotel as it was so convenient and had a good reputation for doing things well. The hotel manager thanked the assistant for the enquiry and said she would get back to him with a price, which in due course she did.

When the assistant heard the hotel's proposed price he was shocked, but not as much as the Perceptive CEO.

'How much?' he asked.

'I know,' said the assistant with a shrug. 'I went back three times but they insisted that this is their rock-bottom price.'

'We'll see,' said the Perceptive CEO and asked another member of her team to phone the hotel.

'This time, instead of making the booking in the name of BigCo, tell them the company is called Lilliput Ltd, and let's see what happens,' she instructed.

To the assistant's surprise, the hotel offered a price 20 per cent lower!

The Perceptive CEO gave a knowing smile.

Big names don't always get best value.

 THE SNEAKY ENTREPRENEUR AND THE CAVIAR

A Sneaky Entrepreneur only had a handful of small shops, but he had big plans for expansion. One day, he had a bright idea. He would sell caviar to appeal to upmarket shoppers and make it look as though his shops sold brilliant quality food at really, really low prices! But he had a trick up his sleeve. Instead of buying expensive European caviar he would buy cheaper Chinese caviar at a fifth of the price.

But who cares? the Sneaky Entrepreneur thought to himself, greedily. *I'll just call it caviar and the customers will think it's the expensive stuff.*

The Sneaky Entrepreneur proudly announced to the local press that his shops were selling caviar for a fraction of the price that other shops sold beluga caviar for. How the press sang his praises as they took the marketing at face value. But, when someone who knew all about the true cost of caviar told the press the truth, they felt foolish for having been duped. So did the knowledgeable customers the discount shop was trying to attract. The Sneaky Entrepreneur's shops found themselves with lots of unsold jars!

Be sure that eventually your misrepresentations will be found out.

BONUS FABLE: THE THOUGHTFUL CEO AND SOMETHING FOR NOTHING!

The Thoughtful CEO of the high street chain, BWise, could see that more and more of her customers were shopping online. As a result fewer were coming into her shops. But the cost of running her shops wasn't reduced, it was in fact going up! Lower prices didn't help, they just meant that less money was taken from the reduced amount of goods sold in the shops. New lines didn't help as they could still be bought online. Cutting costs just reduced service in the shops and pushed more people online. More money was spent on advertising to attract new customers, but that just drove people to order more online, which although a less profitable way to sell things was growing fastest of all. And with all of her competitors in the same boat the situation was getting rapidly worse.

I know, thought the Thoughtful CEO, why don't we give our customers something they will value, which costs us very little, they don't get online and will bring them to our shops routinely! The Thoughtful CEO's brilliant Marketing Man had a plan. 'Free coffee and newspapers,' he exclaimed. 'Coffee shops, which are booming, are charging pounds for coffee that costs pennies to make. Newspapers only cost a little too, and I'm sure if the volumes were large we could get a very good deal from the newspaper publishers. I'm sure it would have a bigger impact on bringing people to our shops than adverts would.'

And he was right. Customers flooded to BWise for their free coffee and newspaper. Sales rocketed and so did customer numbers.

Sometimes there is a big difference
between real and perceived cost.

THE ENERGETIC BOSS

When the new boss arrived he was brimming with ideas. New products, more innovation, better prices, greater service, more outlets, better training and so on and so forth. It was like watching a three-ring circus as all areas of the business worked hard, improved, caught up and then overtook the competition. 'Will he never stop!' exclaimed the team as new idea followed new idea. Many yearned for a rest but enjoyed the fruits of their success and the encouragement to try new things.

After the energetic boss left everyone was relieved when the new leader called for a period of 'consolidation'. A time to improve what had been done, to draw breath, to reflect. The pace lessened but so did progress. The competition pushed forward and went from followers to leaders once more.

Running a business is like travelling up a down escalator.
Run and you make progress, walk and you stay the same,
stand still and you go backwards.

THE MACHINE BY MARK PRICE

In the beginning was the idea and the idea was good,
  so good it became a machine.
The machine only exists to make money for
  those who own it.
The machine doesn't care about the consequences of
  its actions if it makes more money.
The machine which hesitates is consumed by another.
The machine doesn't mind being consumed if it
  makes more money for the owners.
The machine demands consistency, order,
  uniformity, process and efficiency.
The machine keeps making new rules and
  ways to check them.
The machine doesn't trust.
The machine gives orders but doesn't explain.
The machine talks to you but you can't talk to it.
The machine has to grow.
The machine demands more each year.
The machine which breaks down has its broken
  parts reused or discarded.
There is a different way...

Taken from 'Fairness for all – unlocking the power of employee engagement.'

SHARE YOUR STORIES

WWW.WORKPLACEFABLES.COM

All of the fables in this book have been drawn from real life – from my own experiences or from hearing about other people's experiences.

We've created **www.workplacefables.com** as a space for people to share their own workplace fables and stories. Visit it and see!

FAIRNESS FOR ALL

Unlocking the power of employee engagement

This is the first time a book has ever explored the unique and much admired model of the John Lewis Partnership. Through looking at it alongside best practice from other companies, Mark Price demonstrates how to help all businesses be more successful.

Delivered in easy-to-digest sections, Part One of the book looks at the principle behind the theory of being employee inclusive whilst Part Two explains how to deliver in practical terms, using the six steps to workplace happiness.

This book focuses on inclusive capitalism, and acting responsibly to all stakeholders is central to this theme, with employees, the most important stakeholders, the drivers of it all. This book is about another way to do things . . . A fairer way . . . A sustainable way.

www.measuringworkplacehappiness.com